V • • V

JOHN FAHEY

Vampire Vultures

DRAG CITY • • CHICAGO

note

IT WAS AN ENTIRELY DIFFERENT EXPERIENCE working on this book than it was to edit John's last book, *How Bluegrass Music Destroyed My Life* (or *Spank One*, as he insists on calling it in these pages). First of all, Ayal Senior did most of the work by painstakingly collecting and arranging the stories. And then, there's the fact that I didn't have the luxury of being able to call John up when I was confused. For example, I couldn't ask him how an unfinished story should end or whether or not he'd meant to misspell a word (because often he had). I'd spent hours with John on the phone determining when he was pushing the boundaries of language for his own purposes and when he had simply made a typo in his haste to get it all down. In the end, I realize it doesn't matter. His writing reflects his wild mind and the energy of his ideas, experiences, and fantasies. Being on John's planet again felt good—and truly inspiring. There was only one John Fahey and now that he's gone, people are still struggling to make sense of how he touched their lives (which is why this short collection has an editor's note, three introductions, and an afterword). Going over these stories felt like visiting someone you thought you'd never see again. And though it's sad that I couldn't call him up on the phone, I sure felt John close by. In fact, right now, I can hear him saying, "Call me Fahey. I hate it when people call me John."

Damian Rogers, FEBRUARY 2003

contents

a word from dr. demento

NO, THIS IS NOT A BIZARRE PRINTING ACCIDENT. . . I, Dr. Demento, purveyor of "Fish Heads," "Dead Puppies," the works of "Weird Al" Yankovic, and other lighthearted musical mischief, am also a disciple of John Fahey. I was actually a Fahey-ite long before I was a Demento. The facts have been recorded elsewhere: I was a fellow student of John's at the UCLA Folk Music Studies program in the mid-Sixties, lived next door to him for a year in Venice (California), acted as "road manager" for a few of John's performing gigs, and shared a lengthy road trip with him in search of old records and traditional musicians.

I'd heard John's music before I met him. When I was at Reed College, another student owned one of the 95 surviving copies of the first pressing of the *John Fahey/Blind Joe Death* LP, John's vinyl debut. I was blown away by John's combination of the two things I loved most in music: traditional blues guitar style and the adventurous harmonies of modern classical music. I think John appreciated some of the things I did for him, but since I was a somewhat orthodox folksong scholar (in those days), I was also part of something he had a problem with. While John loved to talk about music as much as anyone, he had no patience with the anal, obsessive, stifling pedantry that often passed for folksong scholarship, especially as exhibited in the large booklets that come with many LPs of traditional music. The equally large booklets that John wrote for several of his Takoma LPs began, I believe, as satires of this "scholarship." (In one of them you'll encounter "Tree Sloth Man"—that's me.) John's writing soon took on a life of its own. When his musical inspiration flagged for a time later on, John found new outlets for his words...and when his musical muse returned in radical new form in the mid-Nineties, his pen was also re-energized and transformed.

Enter John Fahey's word-world and you'll discover the sting of his sarcasm and his utter disdain for tact, but you'll also realize that there are some things he holds very dear, and he fights for them like a tiger. As storyteller, music critic, or philosopher (or all three at once), he may get you riled up sometimes...which is just what he had in mind. Get as mad as you want...wherever he may be, Fahey will love you for that. Writing this on the day of his death, I realize more than ever what a life-changing experience it was to know John, or at least some part of what he was. While I may not be able to communicate that experience like I wish I could, his words (like his music) say it all.

Barry Hansen, FEBRUARY 22, 2001

introduction

IN 1999, JOHN FAHEY WAS LIVING ALONE in a single motel room along a vague sketch of highway in Woodburn, Oregon. There was no room service and the phone was barely plugged in. Taped to the wall over John's bed was a hex sign he had drawn in fluorescent marker on some construction paper. Creative mental-debris was splattered everywhere. John kept his guitar in the trunk of his car, which had been stuffed with trash that I'd *cleaned out* for him. As a token of his appreciation, he bought me a copy of Iron Maiden's *Piece of Mind* LP at a local Value Village. That August, John invited me to visit him at the Woodburn Motel, and I stayed for a spell in a room down the hall. During the first few days of my visit we shared a playful interest in philosophic syllogism, exquisite corpse games, and music. Then Hitomi arrived.

John confessed to have fallen in love with Hitomi when he played in Japan earlier that year. He sent her a plane ticket, and when she arrived they disappeared for two days, leaving me alone at the motel with the key to John's room. The fallout of paintings, scrapbooks filled with art-collage, half-finished short stories, unsent letters, musings on napkins, etc., had reached critical mass. All the things you would generally expect to find in the room of a reclusive genius living out his last weird days. John encouraged me to sift through his world of word-*merz* and help him compile his notebooks into a work in progress for his second novel. *Vampire Vultures*, or *Spank Two*, would be a pataphysical autobiography in which John leads a rebellion of his childhood friends against a race of aliens called the Krell, who had disguised themselves on earth as humans so they could melt and eat children. John disclosed to me that the book would end in a messianic bloodbath where the Great Koonaklaster, a cosmic entity and personal friend, would lead Fahey and his friends back to Valhalla.

"Vampire Vultures" is the only complete story edited by John in the unfinished Koonaklaster series. Although still in its conceptual stage, this brief book is a unique glimpse into John's alchemy of myth, memoir, correspondence, and prose. At John's request, I have left out the names of those to whom his letters are addressed. Also, to help the reader, an asterisk [*] appears in places where passages end without explanation. Several notebooks were illegible and are not included here. At some point, John became convinced that I should continue to edit and compile his words. Naturally, I was thrilled to be a part of John's world, even if only for a short time. Our music as the Three Day Band with Barry from the Value Village and those two girls we picked up remains unreleased and discrete. John became increasingly reclusive over the next year, a condition exacerbated by his poor health and diet, but he still showed signs of interest in "the project" when we spoke on the phone. Acknowledgments to Barry Hansen, Byron Coley, John Allen, NNCK, and Mitchell Greenhill.

Ayal Senior, MARCH 2002

POEM:

a hymn of scent

john fahey
the great koonaklaster
bound too tight by the universe
just as he was bound too tight
by clothes
& even by skin
(designed to be worn
by a mere mortal)
(which he was not)
has left his meat
empty & untended
but not forgotten
& not unloved

for in the memories
& the future trajectories
of a thousand nights
& of a thousand trips
& of a thousand glides through the aether
his haunting presence
if not quite as big as life
nor quite as smelly as life
still twirls thick fingers
like dark crystals
that refract endlessly
through the roil of eternity

& he gave so much
of himself
& of his, uh, "essence"

that the stain he left
on our planet
which was merely
another sofa
to him
will never be fully erased
no matter
how hard they scrub

Byron Coley, FEBRUARY 2001
DEERFIELD, MA

PROLOGUE:

an exercise in bad taste

WHAT WITH ALL THE ACCLAMATION OVER MY BOOK *Spank One*, the radio and TV interviews, the praise and blame, adulation, controversy, and attacks, I propose to begin *Spank Two* by telling you something about myself and my life which I have not mentioned previously.

One would think that a person such as myself—never terribly unhealthy; not grotesque in appearance; of reasonable intelligence; never poverty-stricken (for long); a person who furthermore has had and continues to have adventures involving cat people, Krell, and various incarnations of God; a person who is well-travelled and reasonably educated; who is said to have a lot of what they call "talent" in the areas of musical composition and performance (which I do not believe I have), painting, writing, scrapbook- and collage-making, not to mention tape-making; a person who may be a bit shy but is hardly a recluse, no, on the contrary, a person who does not like very many people, but adores some people; a person who spent almost ten years in psychoanalysis and learned a great deal about the unconscious; a person, that is to say, who has led a pretty full life and has every reason to expect to continue living in this manner for a few more decades; a person who has "been around"; and a person who thinks, at least, that generally speaking, is aware, let me emphasize that,

AWARE

of what is going on inside him and around him, much more than most people—one would expect such a person to probably say, if asked about his happiness, that he has been happy most of his life and that he is happy right now. That is what one would expect.

Isn't it?

Wouldn't you expect me to tell you that I am happy and have been happy most of my life, hanging around with the Great Koonaklaster, cat people, fighting Krell? As such a person, I ought to be happy. I ought to have always been happy, at least most of the time. However, I wish to engage in a bit of bad taste and bitching right at the beginning of this book, precisely where one ought not to do such an uncouth and unharmonious and even presumptuous thing, and tell you right off that I am not happy and that I have never in all my life been happy. I am gregarious and simple enough to believe that many of you who read this will not only be surprised, but I even believe that many of you will care. Perhaps the main reason I wish to tell you this is because of an ethical desire to be honest with you. After all, I portray myself in these entertainments as a pretty happy guy, and I feel guilty about that, although it was a great deal of fun. To be more precise, I feel that I have betrayed myself. Yes. Definitely. I feel much worse about betraying myself than about betraying you.

I don't mean to insult or anger you.

I want you to know the truth.

Yes, I have been playing the great American happiness game. I have been implying on almost every page that I'm a happy person. That is the way I was brought up, not just by my "family," but by every institution and facet of society.

In my early days as a composer of guitar music, I was under this same influence. Once in a while, I would allow you to have an indisputably melancholy, perhaps violent, death-and-destruction piece.

But in most pieces I would mitigate the underlying and over-whelming

GREAT SAD

by throwing in harmonies and rhythms, etc., which disguised and hid the truth.

And that is what I did much of the time in *Spank One*, and that is what I did in a lot of *Spank Two*, this book that you are reading.

Oh, for the very discerning, I let the cat out of the bag with the gallows humor. With the portraits of injustice, sadism, rape, etc.

Yes, I did that. But I nevertheless feel that in many cases I was disingenuous.

And I want to make this perfectly clear:

I AM NOT NOW, AND HAVE NEVER BEEN, HAPPY.

OK, now I feel better. I have unburdened myself.

I thank you.

And now if you will give me just a little more time, I will tell you why I am unhappy. I trust that there are a sufficient number of caring people out there who want to know why.

You might expect something complex, something profound, something unusual, something appropriate for a character such as myself.

But that is not the case.

The matter is very, very simple, and yet the solution to it has always evaded me.

Here:

I have never had a relationship with a woman that made me happy.

That is why I am unhappy.

Oh, I can make women happy. Some women are absolutely crazy about me.

I am polite, charming, warm, chivalrous, generous, and on-and-on-and-on.

Women have told me this.

Some women have told me other things, of course.

But I have made at least a few women quite happy and supported them emotionally and financially, and well—I don't want to brag.

But I? I have never been happy with any woman.

That's why I am sad. Very sad.

And perhaps that's why I wrote this book. *Maybe that's why* I write and play music. Maybe that is why I paint and do all these artistic things I do. In fact that *is* the reason I do all these things. Let's get rid of the maybe. I am trying to attract someone out there who I can be happy with and who I can make happy.

Well, now that I've told you the truth, I feel much better.

I thank you for allowing me this levity, and so—on with the book. The first section is called:

the spring

I SUPPOSE IT ALL BEGAN WHEN JACKIE SHORT, our gang leader, received a microscope for Christmas one year. Somewhere between 1945 and 1950. Jackie and his brother Jammie lived right across the street from me. I was over there one afternoon, sitting with them under their Christmas tree. Soon the other kids came around, too. Jackie Short, who was my boyhood idol, soon had put the microscope together on top of a sturdy desk. He instructed us all to go out and collect various kinds of water and goo and semi-permeable membranes so that we could *all* look at what was really there in the microcosmos.

So we all went out with buckets and pails and siphons and trowels.

It didn't take us long to collect samples of river water, creek water, swamp water, algae colonies, leaves, and all kinds of stuff from the surrounding neighborhood.

And so Jackie put some river water on a slide and showed it to us.

Boy, were we surprised when we looked through the scope and saw all kinds of previously unknown

CRITTERS

some of which Jackie was able to identify for us, and show us in the family encyclopedia. I don't remember their names. Then we tried some of the creek water and it was the same, only the critters were different. Same with swamp water—different critters, but critters nonetheless. And it was the same with the sections of leaves and mud and algae and so forth.

There were critters everywhere.

Yes.

What an education.

Then Jackie ordered some tap water.

Gosh, there were even a few critters in the tap water.

We thought the chlorine killed off all the critters. But a few survived.

And Jackie identified all of them and explained that none of them were dangerous unless they appeared in much larger numbers.

Then I remembered something.

ME: Hey, we forgot to get some water from the spring in Denny Briss's backyard.

I immediately grabbed a clean bucket and went over to Denny's backyard. (Denny wasn't there with us because he refused to join the gang. The hell with Denny Briss.) Now, we all knew that this spring was kind of unusual, because we had measured the temperature of the water that flowed through it—at quite a fast speed, I might add—and we had measured the temperatures of all the other springs in the neighborhood. We found, to our surprise, that spring water doesn't change very much all year 'round. Never more than ten degrees. An average of five degrees.

Why not?

Nature is nature and has its own rules and games and tendencies, etc.

Doesn't it?

We thought it did anyway.

The problem was that this fine spring, the one in Denny Briss's backyard, never changed temperature. All year 'round, during the hottest summer, in cold midwinter, the temperature was always in stasis.

And everybody in the neighborhood kept a bottle of it at home in their Kelvinators.

It was always clean, it tasted like ambrosia, and well, this seemed, and seems, hard to believe, but everybody said it had healing properties. Whenever anybody got sick, the doctor came and dispensed medicine, just like everywhere else. And everybody healed pretty quickly. And although nobody ever said so out loud, everybody, even me, believed that it was this spring water, not the miracle drugs, that healed people.

Whenever I got sick, my mother brought me some spring water.

It was so delicious—especially when you were all hot and dry with a fever. And soon after you drank some, the fever would start to decline and the disease to abate. And at night, it would help you sleep and you would dream about the spring, and you would dream that you entered into it and that there was a system all around the world, everywhere, with openings, and that you traveled under the ground, through the spring water, and could visit any place you wanted to go, like China or Buchistan or Bilo Russia or Java.

And pretty soon you would be well.

The whole time I lived in Takoma Park, I know this sounds crazy, I never heard of anybody dying.

Maybe somebody did, but...

Anyway, I took the bucket of spring water back to Jackie Short's living room, and he took some of the water out of the pail with an eyedropper, and put it on a slide, and put the slide on the clasp, and lowered the lens, and raised it again.

JACKIE: Hmmm! Nothing. I don't see anything.

Then he squirted the eyedropper out in the waste can and ordered some more.

But the same thing happened again. The stuff was invisible under the scope. So he ordered some river water. Maybe the machine was broken. But no, the scope was OK. There were the same old river-water microbacteria with the same old critters swimming gaily around.

So he tried the spring water again.

Nothing.

And again and again and again. And still nothing.

So he turned to his brother Jammie.

JACKIE: Go down in the basement and bring up the black paint with the brush. Sometimes you have to dye things to seem 'em.

Jammie quickly returned with the black paint and the brush.

JACKIE: OK, Jammie, put the paintbrush in the paint.

Jammie complied.

JACKIE: Now, Jammie, stick the paintbrush in the spring water and stir it around.

So Jammie picked up the paintbrush full of black paint and stuck it into the bucket of spring water. And of course, we all expected the water to turn black.

But it didn't change color at all.

The water stayed the same but the black paint disappeared as soon as it hit the water.

It was then that we knew that we had ahold of something. But what, we didn't know. So, like in all experiments, we repeated the action *again and again*.

But each time the same thing happened. The black paint disappeared.

So Jackie took some of the spring water and put it on a slide.

Nothing. Just nothing.

Yes, we all had ahold of something very unusual. Something that contradicted all the laws of science. This was very disturbing to us since we all planned to be scientists when we grew up. Mad scientists, of course, like Dr. Savannah in *Captain Marvel Adventures*, only *we* really *would* conquer the universe. But in order to be mad scientists, first we had to learn how to be normal scientists.

At least that's what Jackie Short said. But now this spring water was screwing up our plans. And we couldn't have that. We really did plan to take over the universe.

We weren't joking.

But this matter was very disturbing.

• •

Now Mr. and Mrs. Short were from farms near Lynchburg, Virginia. Of course they were very nice, but they didn't know anything about science. But my father subscribed to *Scientific American* and he knew a lot about science. And so did Mr. Fishhead. He worked for the telephone company, and he repaired radios and TV sets in his spare time. So we figured he must know a lot about science, too. So I told my father about it and he came over and repeated the experiment.

Same thing. Nothing.

So my father called up Mr. Fisher on the phone and told him about it.

So Mr. Fisher came over and... same damned thing.

So my father and Mr. Fisher started discussing it.

MR. FISHER: You know, Al, they have an electron microscope over at the physics department at MDU. I wonder if they would examine it for the kids if we called them up.

MY FATHER: Let's try it. Why not? I'll do the talking.

My father was good at talking so he got the phone book and looked up the number. He called up over there in College Park and told them the story and asked if us kids could bring the water over and if they'd look at it on the electron microscope. My father said they sounded very interested and that we could take it over any weekday in the morning and that they'd examine it.

So early the next week we took the water over to MDU, and found the physics building, and eventually found the guys my father had talked to. They took the water. They wouldn't let us near the electron microscope, but they started fooling around with it and the water.

• •

After about 15 minutes:

"Hey, what the hell? There's nothing there! What is this, some kind of joke? Those kids are playing a goddamn joke on us."

And then they came running down the hall and chased us out of the building and told us never to come back.

What the hell can you do?

Especially when you're a kid. Nobody wants to believe you.

[*]

can you understand me?

Dear T.,

Now I am on American Airlines D.C. 6 (??). I had to sit in the verdamnt airplane for two hours because the weather was bad at Chicago-O'Hare. Can you understand me? Your English was excellent, I thought. I was very sad to see you hurry off with the other women and not look back. I am one of the best experimental-alternative guitarists in the world. While in Tokyo, I met K. Haino, who I have heard many times on CD making noise in a black cape. When I met him in Tokyo, however, he was dressed up in a coat of very funny contrasting, conflicting colors. He looked like a friendly little elf! He was very funny. We discussed the possibility of making a CD together. Now what is happening in the cultural vultural sound scene is this: There is less and less noise happening here in Japan and all over the world. I gave up noise. I only play music now. But it is very good and very unusual music. Most of it is very angry and sad and very beautiful, I think. Mostly I write my own music. I am going to suggest to Haino that we do an album of music together. I hope he doesn't get mad at me.

Yours,
J.F.

prolegomena to all questions regarding cat people, past, present, and future

ONE TIME IN THE HOT SUMMER, I walked down the Baltimore and Ohio RR tracks to the place where you can climb down the vine-covered hill of train ash and arrive either in front of Youngblood's Hardware or on the side of Rinaldi's Entertainment Center.

That's where the pool hall was. That's where I was heading.

But as I approached the front door, I saw a cat person across the street in front of Troll's Bakery hailing me with a hex sign and motioning me to come over.

I was always polite to cat people. And to cats as well. I knew the cat people lived in forests and were very poor and were separatists and that everybody had to be nice to them. Not just because of charity, but because if the cat people ever went away from the Sligo River Valley basin, fleas and other insects and rodents as well would return to our valley and ruin the crops and spread black plague and pink eye and gingivitis and all kinds of terrible diseases.

So I was always very nice to cat people whenever I saw them.

The cat people spoke English as well as Cat and Sanskrit.

I don't know where they learned it, but...

I mean, when you think about it, the cat people were here in this valley long before the coming of human beings.

The Great Kelvinator, who had created the Sligo River Valley for his special people, which was most of us, willed it that way.

And who among us is wise enough to question the motives and ambitions of the Great Kelvitron?

Certainly not me.

The cat person opened his mouth and spoke to me:

"Big Cat come tonight. You come too. Come to Spring Park."

"What are you talking about?" I asked. "What cat, what big cat?"

"You come Spring Park tonight, you find out. Tell the others. Everybody come to Spring Park tonight and see Big Cat come."

"Ah, OK, sure. I'll come tonight and I'll tell the others, too. No problem."

"Thank you," said the cat person. "Thank you."

Then I saw him accosting somebody else.

Everybody, including myself, was always very polite to the cat people, because we had been taught to be that way by our parents, by our churches and synagogues, and by the Elks and the CIA and all the other organizations in our little town. The cat people were very poor and lived in seclusion somewhere near the Great Sligo River on the north side where the Pyramids are somewhere in the back of the swamp. They were separatists who had their own religion and wished to live quietly by themselves and practice their rituals alone and secretly. The cat people were hardly seen and never tried to convert anybody to cat-people-ism. In fact, they hardly ever came into town at all, and when they did come, they were usually alone for some reason. Once every other year or so, they came to tell us regular human beings that they were starving and ask if we could collect some food for them at the churches and mosques. Or that they were having some epidemic and that they needed doctors and medicine since they had none themselves.

The custom of helping the cat people was so old that nobody

could remember when it started. And we were all taught—and we all believed—that we must always treat the cat people well and always help them when they were in trouble, because somehow our welfare was tied up with the fortune of the Great Sligo River Valley dwellers and the fertility of the alluvial plane, which is situated on the south side of the Great Sacred River where the Pyramids were. And of course, it was well known that there were no mice or rats or fleas in the Sligo River Basin, and many people assumed that the cat people's presence and magical rituals effected the total absence of these nefarious rodents and insects.

But the cat people never told us that.

These beliefs were traditions that were older than the hills.

Anyway, I told the people in the pool hall and my parents and everybody else who I saw that day to be at Spring Park that night.

And so that night at about 7:30, we all walked over to see what was up.

Well, there were a great many people at Spring Park. No cat people, but plenty of regular people. And everybody was speculating about what it was that the cat people wanted us there for.

Then a few cat people showed up, walking up from the river.

At that point, something clicked. I asked my parents if there was a development plan scheduled by one of the big land developers.

"Well, yes," my father replied. "There is a plan by the Sand and Gravel Company to build a big-ass shopping center out there and several large housing developments."

"Do the cat people live as far north as the Patuxant River?" I asked my father.

"I thought they all lived down here. I never heard about any entering Skaggsville or Ellicot City," he said.

"Maybe they shouldn't," I suggested.

"Maybe not," he said. Let's wait and see what this 'Big Cat' deal is all about."

"Do you suppose," I asked my father, "that when the cat people say 'Big Cat' they are actually talking about some real cat that's real big that they worship back there in the swamps?"

"I dunno," my father answered. "There's a hell of a lot of land between the Sligo and the Patuxant rivers. And swamps and tributaries. There are no maps of the area except ones made from photographs taken from airplanes flying over that land, and a lot of those photographs are very ambiguous and unclear."

"I hear that nobody goes exploring or fishing or hunting north of the Sligo River because a long time ago a few people went hunting terrestrial muskelunge up there but none of them ever came back. So now nobody goes there."

"Yes, that's what I heard, too," said my father. "I'm never gonna go up there. Might be anything."

"How many miles is it between the Sligo and the P.?"

"Must be at least 40 miles," said my father. At least at this latitude. As you get closer and closer to the Bay, the distance diminishes, of course, because at Point Potreglie the Sligo empties into the P. And that's 60 miles east. So it's like an isosceles triangle. Let's see what the formula is...

"Gosh, Chonney," my father said, "that's ____ miles square. I never thought about it before, but those cats, if what they say is true about having a land grant from the Great Koonaklaster, own enough land to equal almost half the size of the state of Maryland."

"Gosh, how I love to hear that name."

"So do I, son," said my father. "There's nobody like Great K. Nobody."

"I know. He speaks to me in the form of the Great Factory PEPCO at night and shows me his face."

"The Great Koonaklaster can appear in many forms, maybe in any form, I dunno," said my father.

"Eddie, across the street, met him once," I added. "He made Eddie a cherry soda with vanilla ice cream. Eddie said it was the best-tasting soda he ever had and that the Great Koonaklaster appeared to him out of a Koonaklaster hex sign, but that he also appeared to Eddie as a nice man, too, a soda jerk, in fact."

"Yes, I heard about that," said my father. "Divine soda jerk. Maybe you and I will see Great K., too. Maybe he'd give us a divine ice-cream soda. Wouldn't that be something, Chonney?"

"It sure would, Dad. It sure would."

"Someday, the Great Koonaklaster, Chonney."

"Someday, in the great all, together, someday in the great all and all."

"Hooray for the Great Koonaklaster! Everybody in the park! Hooray, hooray, three cheers for the Great Koonaklaster!"

And we all got very happy just hearing Great K.'s name, because after all, the Great Koonaklaster is incarnate in his name. We all got so happy that we started dancing around and chanting:

> KOONAKLASTER KOONAKLASTER
> KELVINATOR KELVINATOR
> CYCLOTRON CYCLOTRON
> MAHA MANTRA MAHA MANTRA
> INCARNATION INCARNATION

After dancing for about half an hour, we all got tired and sat down on the slightly damp grass and let ourselves be cooled by the soft winds coming up from the Chesapeake Bay. The sun had gone down long ago and it was pretty dark. Then, abruptly, the moon came out, and as it did we saw dozens of lions and tigers and ocelots and pumas coming out from the south, walking in amongst us, all purring quietly and peacefully. Here and there, one curled up in somebody's lap or started rubbing against somebody. Nobody was scared, of course, because these were all obviously tame, human-loving wildcats, and besides we were all protected because we had just been chanting and dancing to the Koonaklaster chant, and we knew that no harm could come to us. The giant cats sat down with us and most of them started washing themselves with their paws and saliva, just like ordinary house cats do.

And the great PURRING was very, very relaxing.

Then, suddenly, all the cats let out a loud roar and stood up facing north and looking at Mount Washington Hill. And without knowing why, all of us humans also stood up and stared at the top of Mount Washington Hill.

And then, in the semi-darkness, we all saw it. There on top of

Mount Washington sat a giant cat, a cat as big as the Azalea City Unitarian Church on Peach Street. This monster cat—we couldn't tell what color he was because the moonlight just wasn't bright enough to make his markings visible to us—all that this giant cat did, like most cats, was sit there on his hind legs and purr, oblivious to everything and everybody else in the world.

Cats, as you know, are the most narcissistic animals on the planet.

They are even more narcissistic than human females.

Big Cat's purr was pretty loud. And as he purred, all the other cats purred, and not just all the other cats, but all of us people started purring, even though very few of us had ever purred before.

Of course, for some reason, I purred all the time when nobody was listening.

And I wasn't the only one.

Sometimes, I fantasized that I was part cat person, but of course, that's impossible.

Isn't it? But all of us, white, black, Oriental, and cat, just sat there and PUUUUUUUUUUUUUUUUUUUUUUUUUUUUUURRRRRRRRRRRRRRR-RRRRRED.

And of course the ground shook. But not much. And the overall effect was calming and relaxing.

And then, gradually, a new voice came into our heads. Not into our hearts, but into our heads, telepathically. A smooth, deep, liquid, warm voice. This was no paltry *meooowww*. This was a godlike, deep voice that seemed to come out of the ground and sounded like the earth itself.

BIG CAT: I am well pleased with your purring tonight, my people. All of you have been so kind and considerate to my children, the cat people, feeding them and caring for them in the winter when I must hibernate and cannot attend to their needs. Be assured, oh people of the Sligo River Valley, that I am aware of your deeds, especially regarding my children, the people of the cat. Indeed I am aware of all your deeds just as my master, the

Great Koonaklaster is. Fear not that your prosperity and peace will end. Fear not that rodents and insects will appear in the Sligo River Valley. Fear not for the fertility of your soil and of your animals and of yourselves. Fear nothing my people. But always remember what the Great Koonaklaster wrote on your hearts:

BE KIND TO A CAT. ANY CAT.
FOR ALL CATS ARE EQUAL IN MY EYES
AND IN GREAT K.'S EYES.

I go now to hunt rodents in the starry heavens. I came tonight to warn you against allowing any land developers to cross the Sligo River and build any houses north of it. This land was ceded to me by Great K. himself. This is only a polite warning. But I must tell you that human beings who are not simply visiting cat people, as friends, are not welcome on the north shore of the Sligo River, and if any non-friendly people are seen there, they will not be seen again by human eyes. That is the way of the Great Kelvinator. In his hands I am nothing but a tiny kitten. And so are you humans. Great K. is not a wrathful god, but...And now I must away to my nocturnal pursuits. I bid you farewell. And remember,

BE KIND TO A CAT.

But those were not the last words Great Cat spoke.

No.

He said one more thing. Something we did not understand at the time.

Something that was not merely ambiguous.

No. It was something that at the time was completely meaningless.

Meaningless, at least to us ordinary human beings.

Yes.

BIG CAT: Do not think that there is any ontological or teleological separations between you humans and us cats. Do not think that, for a Great War is coming and many cat people will die for your sakes. Many, many, many of my most ardent disciples are going to give their lives and go onto the battlefields beside you and freely and intentionally lay down their lives for you. Please, therefore, be kind to a cat, for greater love hath no man or cat known than he who lay down his life for a man or a cat. Now I bid you adieu.

[*]

the blue mead notebook

KRSNA, THE BLUE FLUTE PLAYER, sings songs within me eternally.
And he dances.

He is always dancing and prancing around and around and up and
down and inside.

Inside.

Always smiling, smiling just for me. Every smile I see, any place I
go—I know that it is Krsna's smile. There is no other smile.

Krsna is the smile your brother beams at you every morning.

Krsna is the look of happiness on your mother's face when she
tucks you into bed at night and says, "Goodnight now, may
your dreams be merry."

Krsna is the smile on your father's face when you learn to ride a
horse and he sees you galloping through the fields of the new-
moon dragon-wart woods.

Krsna is the smell of new-moon hay.

Krsna's piping is the song you sing when the wind whispers to you
in the night season.

Krsna is the sound you hear in the winter wind blowing through
the sleeping dry oak, hydrangea bushes all stiff and tough.

Krsna is the sound of wind chimes, far out in the Mojave Desert,

whispering in the dark night when I am dreaming about you.
The sound I cannot hear.

But I know it's there. I know it.

Just as I know you. K. told me about you.

K. told me about you. I like the rhythm.

I knew him before I saw his blue.

I knew Krishna before I met him.

I knew him before I met you. I knew you before—long before.

I remember K. I remember you.

Do you remember me? I was there!

K.'s blue spills itself all over the world and paints the sky.

A symbol of K.'s ever presence.

The white of the clouds are K.'s purity.

And the purity of the lover on K.

K. is the bluegrass of Kentucky.

K. is the blue of the angelfish in the seven seas.

K. is the big blue sea.

K. is my love for you.

K. is the blue ribbon you gave to me in your dream.

K. plays the magic flute.

Once the Jimuna river was blue. But the government diverted
much of the water for irrigation.

Kali Juga.

The cycle is almost over. Almost begun anew. The end is in sight.

Time is ending in me.

The very last taboos had to be broken. I broke them in my book.

They matter no longer.

But perhaps I am deceived by a demon and it is not you who calls
me.

K. is the promise of the springtime. I see flowers in the rainbow.

Your opulent nectar is calling me.

Cross-pollination.

K. keeps the kite I fly aloft.

You are so much closer to Krishna than I am.

You are in the purity which I crave.

Please come, or call me to you.

If not now, then when the blue says to. Plenty of time.
Forever and ever.
Let's jump into the blue vortex.
It won't be long till the curtains fall at the Grand Finale.
I want to be with you until then.
Don't wait. You might be too late.
Don't take any chances.
I want you here.
And who am I?
Nobody. I was never here.
Annihilated by you. My past an illusion.
Annihilated by you.
I know who you are. Why do you think I followed you around?
Don't you know me? You could teach me so much.
I was happy till I went to Houston. Now I am so miserable. My
    happiness no longer exists except in you. I want you to come up
    here and stay with me permanently.
Are you coming or not?

Thank You

a lovers' triangle

H.A., Dear Sir,

I apologize for any discomfort or emotional pain that I may have caused in regards to your lovely wife, H. I do not have the intention of hurting anyone. Nevertheless, this situation has arisen in which "a lovers' triangle" does, in fact, exist between H., you, and me. Let us not speak of ancient, outmoded religious concepts such as "right and wrong," or "good and evil," except insofar as they are embodied in law. Let us speak rather of happiness. Who is more important? You? Me? What about H.? Is not H.'s happiness more important than your happiness and mine?

Let us be perfectly clear. I do not want to fight or argue with you. I would prefer to be your friend. This is possible for me. Is it possible for you? H. says she is not happy with you. H. says she is happy with me. Once again, I ask you, whose happiness is more important?

Yours?

Mine?

H.'s?

If you are worried and/or are concerned about H., I wish to

assure you that I take excellent, the best care of H. I am an honor-able man, just as I am certain you are.

I love H. I adore H. I want only happiness for her. Let us both be honorable. Leave H.'s decision up to her. Let us both allow her the freedom of happiness.

J.F.

our end is in our beginning

ONE DAY WHEN I WAS ABOUT 13, Dorothy Gooch, my longtime girlfriend, walked all the way over from Prince George's County to see me. That was about five miles. And it was hot and humid. The sun beat down on our little town all day. It beat down on the trees and the cats and the dogs and the box turtles and the alligator snapping turtles and the garter snakes and the cypress trees and the people young and old.

It wasn't that big a deal for Dorothy to walk that far to my house or for me to walk that far to hers. There was no public transportation and we were both too poor to have cars or bicycles. So we walked.

She found me in the backyard resting in the shade.

I didn't even get up. She didn't expect me to. It was too hot.

She plumped herself down beside me.

DOROTHY: Something's come up. I had to come over and find you.

ME: That's cool, Dorothy. You can come over to see me anytime you want. You know that.

DOROTHY: Yeah. I guess I do know that.

ME: You're my girlfriend, Dorothy. And we're in the same gang.

You can come see me whenever you want to.

DOROTHY: OK, I will. But I have to tell you something.

ME: Shoot.

DOROTHY: Do you remember Father Hurbitz at the CYO dances at Our Lady of Sorrows?

ME: Sure, I remember Hurbitz. He's a nice guy. He's always speaking in metaphors. Anybody who likes metaphors is OK by me.

DOROTHY: Yeah, he is a nice guy.

ME: So?

DOROTHY: Johnny, Father has cancer real bad. He's probably going to die.

ME: Ah hell, that's a shame. I like him.

DOROTHY: Everybody likes Father Hurbitz. He's a saint. He's always helping people and he never says anything bad about anybody and...

ME: I know. He's a great guy.

DOROTHY: Johnny, you remember one time you told me there was some funny water in a spring around here somewhere? You said sometimes it cures people.

ME: Hell, it always cures people. I didn't used to believe it when I was younger, but now I do. It never fails. It's healed me from mumps and flu and things lotsa times.

DOROTHY: Where is it? Can I see it?

ME: Oh, the spring's right across the street in Denny Briss's backyard.

DOROTHY: I told Father about it and he asked me to come and get some of it from you.

ME: Oh, sure. No problem. Let's get a bucket and scrub it out and we'll take some over to him.

DOROTHY: He'll be really happy if we do that for him, Johnny. Even if it doesn't work. He...

ME: Oh, it'll work. Don't worry. It'll work.

DOROTHY: How can you be sure?

ME: I didn't used to believe in the stuff myself, until I got really sick a few times. I had a raging fever that the doctors and their penicillin couldn't stop. I was really ready to make the big, long crossover. And then I started dreaming about the spring across the street and the water in it. You know, that water is the same temperature all year 'round. We did a bunch of experiments on it with Jackie Short's microscope and all. Every other kind of water showed up under Jackie's microscope, but not that spring water. We tried river water, creek water, swamp water, and tap water, and there were these critter-like amoebae and things in all those kinds of water, but nothing showed up in the spring water on Jackie's scope! That water was invisible.

DOROTHY: Oh, come on...

ME: No really. We put dye in it and everything and put it under the scope! Nothing. We took the water out to the chemistry department at the University of Maryland, and they put it under an electron microscope. Nothing.

DOROTHY: What's an electron microscope?

ME: Hell, I dunno. A microscope made out of electrons, I guess. Much more powerful than a regular microscope. But nothing. The professors got mad at us and chased us out of the building. They thought we were playing a trick on them. I'd like to know how to play a trick like that. Anyway, when I was sick, damn near dead, I asked my mother to go over and get me some. Most of the people around here take some of that water when they get sick. And you know, nobody has died here since we moved out here five years ago and discovered it.

DOROTHY: Wow. Maybe it'll help Father Hurbitz.

ME: Oh it will, it will. It might take a few days to cure him, but as soon as he drinks some of it, he'll start to get better. You wait and see.

DOROTHY: Where does this magic come from? Where does it go?

ME: I don't know where it goes or where it comes from. Maybe someday I'll find out something about it. All I know is I started drinking it when I had that fever and it was gone in a few days. Since then I've drank some every day, three times a day, and I've never been sick once.

DOROTHY: Not once?

ME: Not once.

DOROTHY: Gosh.

So we went down in my basement and got a bucket and washed it out and then went and filled the bucket about half-full with the spring water. I knew that if we'd fill it to the brim we'd spill it. And we didn't want to do that.

DOROTHY: Will you walk me over to Our Lady of Sorrows? It's kinda heavy and it's awfully hot out.

ME: Why, Dorothy, I wouldn't think of letting you carry this all the way over to the church on your own. You gotta remember you're my girlfriend. I like to help you.

DOROTHY: I'm sorry I keep forgetting, Johnny. But people were so mean to me before I met you, making fun of me all the time because they all knew what my father was doing to me. It's just real hard believing way down deep that somebody really cares about whether I live or die. Or what happens to me.

ME: Yeah. It's rough. My father, you know...

DOROTHY: Sometimes I'm happy, especially when I think about you and how you beat up my father and told him never to bother me again. And you know, he never has bothered me again since you bashed him.

ME: Yeah, I really gave it to him and promised him a lot more if I ever heard from anybody that he was bothering you again. He'll never forget.

DOROTHY: I still don't understand why you decided to be nice to me and protect me. I don't know if I'll ever understand why you like me. I don't like myself.

ME: Don't you like yourself even a little bit when we're together? Aren't you a little happy with me?

DOROTHY: Oh yes, Johnny, I'm always happy when I'm with you, or when I think about you, or especially when we go to the park after the movies. I'm always happy then.

ME: Dorothy, maybe it's because I'm always happy when I'm with you, or when I'm thinking about you, and I know that you know that I'm thinking about you and that I'm happy, especially because I know you're happy ever since I took care of your father. And those kids who were teasing you all the time and making you miserable.

DOROTHY: Do you really think about me that much Johnny?

ME: Yes, Dorothy. I think about you all the time. See, you don't see how beautiful you are. You don't see your humility. You don't see how good you are inside, even though all those people raped you and teased you and beat you up for so long. No, you don't see that. But I see it. And I feel it. And you're a really wonderful person, Dorothy. You're ten times as good as any of those people that were making you feel so bad. And I know it takes a long time for you to change how you feel about yourself. Oh, I know how you see yourself. But it's gradually going away, that old picture of yourself. And a new picture's growing inside you. And that picture is like the one I have of you. And I have the true genuine photograph of the true Dorothy Gooch. And I know someday you'll have it too.

DOROTHY: Uhh…

ME: Yeah, I know it's hard for you, see, but here's the thing you gotta remember: Whenever you start to worry, especially if it's about me, remember it doesn't bother me. Maybe it bothers you. But it doesn't bother me away from you. And that's what you're really worried about. You're afraid I'll leave you or drop you for some other girl for something or other. I don't know what. But I told you I'd never leave you, and I meant it, and I swear to you, I never-never-never will leave you. I'll always be here for you and nobody else. And I'll always love you and take care of you. See, Dorothy, there's something else about you that you're not aware of. And there's something in the future that's very important about you. I don't know what it is, but sometimes I dream about it—almost—always with symbols, pictures, not pictures of the real thing, but pictures anyway. And they are very important pictures I get in my dreams. And sometimes when I'm awake, I see it. I almost see it. But I can't tell you much about it, because I don't understand what it is myself.

DOROTHY: Sometimes I don't understand you, Johnny. I don't get what you're talking about. But I trust you, Johnny. I really trust you. And you know that I love you. You know that, don't you?

ME: Yes, Dorothy. I do know that way down deep. I knew the first time I met you and we went to the Allen. You had hoped for me, somebody like me, who would see you the way I see you. And would love you. And you waited for years and years and nobody had showed up and you were beginning to doubt and you were coming on despair and you were scared. But as soon as you saw me, you knew it was me. And it was the same for me with you. I knew it right away. And I didn't give a damn what those outlanders had done to you or what they thought about you. It didn't even make an impression on me.

I SAW YOU THE WAY YOU REALLY ARE.

And nobody had ever done that before. And we both knew it, and we both fell into each other's arms. Remember?

DOROTHY: I'll never forget.

ME: Yeah, you'd better not forget.

And so we walked down the streets of Takoma Park in the hot, wet sun, carrying the bucket of magic water for Father Hubritz. And we talked about ourselves and our relationship, which was so unusual at such a young age. I was only 13 and she was 12. But she didn't look like she was 12. She grew up fast. Maybe it was all the suffering and the poverty. I don't know, but the first time I saw her, I knew I was doomed. My heart was wounded and so was hers.

Consequently, everything else was trivial to us. We never had arguments because compared with our obsession nothing was worth fighting about.

We saw other couples fighting all the time. But we never argued. Not once.

It simply never happened that Dorothy wanted to do something different than what I wanted to do. Oh, there were preferences, of course, but we were both always willing to give into the other person if it seemed like their wants were stronger or more important. And the fact is, at a very early age, we enjoyed giving our wills away to the other. I enjoyed doing whatever Dorothy wanted to do rather than what I wanted to. (We didn't know it at first, but we were receiving help and direction and many other virtues from a person who we had not yet met. Not in person that is. But we met the Great Kelvinator in our dreams every night. And he was becoming a part of us more and more, bit by bit, every day. And yet neither one of us knew anything about him.)

Late that afternoon, we arrived at the church on Ethan Allen Avenue and one of the nuns took us and our bucket of magic water to Father Hubritz's quarters. His room wasn't very large and there wasn't much of anything in it. A chair. A small table. A mirror. Some crucifixes.

In those days the religious still used crucifixes.

Maybe he had a radio. I forget. But there was no TV set.

Father lay upon his bed under his sheet. He was sweating like a pig. He was skinnier than I had ever seen him before. He didn't have much hair, but the hair he did have was white as snow. He had a mustache and a small pointed beard. Everything about him was a whisper. A diminution. He was even shrinking physically.

But when he saw Dorothy and me and our bucket, he smiled. And he looked at us straight in the eyes when he spoke to us. His eyes were very blue. Not steely blue, but sea blue. Deep, wet, and alive. Very alive. Oh, the rest of him might be dying of cancer or some infection, but Father Hubritz was still very much there in his strong deep blue eyes.

And then he spoke. He was still very much alive in his mind.

And though he spoke only in a whisper that first day, his words were and still are perfectly clear and kind and even loving.

There was no confusion in that man.

He was in his eighties then. He had spent his entire life fighting for the thing he believed in, and that was the Church. The Church was no building, he explained. The Church was the body of Christ.

ME: I don't understand.

FATHER: Oh, yes you do, John m'boy. You understand, but you don't know that you understand.

ME: What is it that I understand, Father?

FATHER: You understand many things, and in the future you will understand many, many more things, things which very few people even think about, much less know about. But I'll tell you one thing you know today, and once I have told you that you will suddenly discover that you have known it all along. Here it is. Ready?

ME: Yes, Father.

FATHER: You, John, my son, understand that the Church is Jesus Christ. You understand that the two are identical. There are no differences whatsoever. And I am not merely talking about essence. Now tell me, my son, do you know that?

And you know what? I did know that. It had never played a very important part in my life, but I had always known it.

ME: Yes, Father, I do know that. I've always known that.

FATHER: And you know what it means, too, don't you?

ME: Yes, Father. I know exactly what it means. I always have.

FATHER: But do you know how you know it, John?

ME: No, I don't know that. Is that important?

FATHER: No, not really. But I'll tell you anyway. You received much of this knowledge when you were baptized. And gradually in another manner also. Mainly through baptism, but the rest will come clear to you as you grow older. Don't worry about whether it is important to you or not or if you want to please me by thinking about it so we could talk about it or something. That isn't important. I simply wanted to point it out to you that you do know what few others know. Perhaps after I'm gone, nobody... But you will know that Jesus Christ and His Church are one and the same. You talk to me, you are talking to Jesus Christ. I talk to your very holy friend Dorothy, I am talking to Jesus Christ. The maid out in the hall is Jesus Christ. We are all Jesus Christ. Not emanations of him, not...no, we are all Jesus Christ.

What was I supposed to do? Thank him for this insight? What should I say? He was always ahead of me.

FATHER: Do not fear talk or conversation with me or with anyone. You need not say anything. Silence truly is golden. The less you speak the better. I know that you are not a gossipmonger or a big talker and that you feel a bit inferior to all that. Forget all that. Keep silent until the time comes to talk. You will always know when the time is the right time. Dorothy, come here, I want to have some words with you.

Dorothy went over to his bedside and he spoke to her very intimately.

In a way, this was Dorothy's real father.

I sat and looked out the window and averted my concentration.

After a while, Dorothy gently put her hand on my shoulder and said Father wanted to talk to me again.

FATHER: I know about this water. I know where it comes from and where it goes and what it is for. I thank you for bringing it to me for I know that it will cure me in short order. It is not time for me to go yet.

He had great faith in it, and I told him he would probably be better in a few days.

FATHER: Yes. Thank you again, son John. I believe you are quite right. Listen, in days to come, you will learn much more about that water and you are about to have some very exciting adventures. You and Dorothy do have a mission in life. I don't know much more about it than you two, but Dorothy has told me her fantasies and feelings and told me yours, too. I hope you don't mind...

ME: Not at all.

[*]

i get tired of pretending i'm a kid

Dear J.,

Life for me has become intolerable. I have turned into some kind of vicious flabby substance, like jelly, including "my mind." (I suppose it is a combination of

AGING

and the horrible chemicals I have taken every day for diabetes and restless leg syndrome. I'm not even sure about that.) I used to know what I wanted and what I didn't want. And I could make decisions easily. It is becoming increasingly difficult for me to make any kind of decision. I am ambivalent about too many things. I shift back and forth like a wind shear.

Business and music decisions...I make these on the basis of conventional wisdom, experience, and a number of advisors, especially my new manager, Dean Blackwood in Nashville. Even here, in the music business, where things have been picking up fast, I am confused a lot. But in personal relations, I am and have been terribly confused for a long time. I didn't really notice this till I got back here from Berkeley last time I saw you. (The Grossman thing.) Then, when I realized how confused I was, especially my feelings about some people, including you, I became terrified.

I saw that my indecisiveness and ambivalence had hurt you. I was so frightened of myself that I shut up like a clam. I was afraid to write back to you after I sent you the tape collage and received your letter.

Since then things have gotten much worse and because of my confusion I have hurt other people as well. Some of them I don't care about. Some of them are the parasitical people who follow me around. They all want money and I give it to them. Then I get pissed off when I can't pay the rent, for example, and I tell them, "No more money!" Then they go away. Fine, I don't care about them. They are not friends. But I have also hurt friends like you and a few others because I keep turning hot and cold. And I can't help it. It's getting worse and worse. At the same time, though, you have never been explicit about what, if anything, you want from me. And I feel bad about that. And then the next day I don't feel anything bad or good about it. This must be a state of degeneration. But why it is happening and what it is, I have no idea. And I am losing control of it more and more. It is progressive. I'm afraid because I'm being driven by contradictory, internal forces over which I have no control.

I do not believe that I hurt you—or anybody else—with deliberation. Sometimes—like when we went record collecting—I was afraid of you, because I believe you come from a higher social class than me. And I felt stupid and inferior. And once or twice I got mad at you because I saw that you were a stronger person than I am and I played one-upmanship with you, especially in the field of psychology. I'm also afraid of you because you're so much more intelligent than me, even though I also admire you and respect you for that. I am also unfairly mad at you because I cannot figure out whether the ambivalence is coming from me or you or from both of us. I cannot figure out why it exists and what causes it. And you wear stunning clothes that only rich Unitarians and Episcopalians wear, even though you look great.

Please don't think that you're the only person I am confused about. I am confused about everybody I know. I mean, anybody who is significant to me. But I even get confused about who is significant to me. I finally met some nice people up here. I spent all day with Tim who owns Guitar Castle and Alisa who works for him on Saturdays. Now Tim really likes and admires me and we help each other. We formed a space rock band with another guy, Rob, who also likes and admires me. Yet no matter what I do, I cannot come to like Tim even though he is great to me. Though lately, I have come to adore Tim and Rob—see what I mean?! Rob is more the intellectual type and he also admires me and I like him, even though he is pretty naïve about music, people, and audiences. In the morning, before I saw her, I was passionately in love with Alisa. By dinner, I realized that the Alisa I was in love with at 10 a.m. didn't even exist. And what about the new one? Am I in love with her? I don't know. Nothing but confusion. (7/17: Turns out she is cruel and sadistic.)

Yes. I think the space music we make—from 100,000 A.D.—is great. Yes. And it will probably sell. But is it important? (7/17: No. But that's OK.)

My previous record, mistitled *City of Refuge*, is, I believe, the best record I ever made (no ambivalence).

I think it is even prophetic.

But this space music I am ambivalent about.

The John Fahey Trio. They gave it the name. They are talented. (Sometimes I have to get bossy, but not very often.) All these guys are 20 years younger than me.

There is a big problem here.

I get tired of pretending I'm a kid.

I get sick of it.

But alternative kids are where my new market is. They leave musical and noise doors open. Unfortunately, older people closed a lot of doors a long time ago and they want me to play the same damned music I did 40 years ago. Nuts. When they put pressure on me to "live in the past," I am rude to them. They walk out. Fine. For every old fart I lose, I gain 20 kids. I am not taking advantage of these kids. I am teaching them a lot. I do chase the young skirts, but I never get anywhere.

Nowhere. But I cannot feel young unless I have a young skirt. But in order to acquire one I have to expend 20 times as much energy. And now I am exhausted from trying to fascinate Alisa all day long. And I don't like the fact that I wasted all that energy on somebody I had misconceived. But if I try to stop fascinating her, it won't work out and next Saturday I will do it again.

I am out of control. Driven.

Playing in a band is a new experience for me. We have recorded some great stuff. (All enclosed.) But it is inhuman music. It contains no emotions. (7/17: Not true.)

Most of alternative is precisely that. An attempt to turn yourself into a machine. Previously in alternative music, I managed to keep it human and emotional minus sentimentality. There was always a lot of that in my music. And cosmic too. I took all that out. Cosmic sentimentality. Transcendental nature feelings too. I was clever. But that's all. "Sunflower River Blues," etc., à la Emerson, Copland. Bullshit. Clever, nothing else. Lies. Nothing but lies.

I didn't know it back then.

I have a gig at the Great American Music Hall in June. Same bill as Kottke. I hate him. But I am only going to attack "The Lake Wobegon Show." It is a lie and it is racist. There is a war going on between alternative and "New Age" in its death throes. Kottke doesn't know this. I'll try to bring a band with me. There!! I wrote a whole letter to you with no smokescreen. See! I can do it. Thank you for pointing this out to me in your last letter. You are probably right and I feel good about it too. I hope to see and hear from you soon. Confused or not, I am finally honest with you.

P.S. OK, now here's the thing. I just figured it out. If you want a lot from me you can have it all. But if you only want a little, you can't have it. I want a lot from you.

Not a little. A lot. Is that clear? I don't see how I could be more clear.

carnation, sleep & dream

Dear C.,

The sparkling clarity of this production does not present or express the depths of the personality or soul or emotions of the real C. In fact, the clarity and positivity are overbearing. There is no mystery. No ambiguity, no ambivalence. I would not bother to critique this production unless I did not feel that you are my friend and that you have a lot of potential. I do not use the word "talent" because I do not believe it exists. I don't have any talent. I suspect you are the victim of

BANDWAGON EFFECT.

A few friends discover that you can sing and play guitar and they turn into a rah-rah section of cheerleaders, screaming, shouting, *Wow wow wow, ain't she great?* Such people are extremely dangerous. Always ask, "What don't you like about it?" I proffered a few critical words and everybody told me to shut up. There are no shadows here. No dangers of solitude. No degrees of anything. It's like the striking naïve sunlight on the Mediterranean beaches. No depths of the northern deciduous forests. Or the sense of smallness and knowledge of one's insignificance when you stand on the

Russian steppes and look out at the endless grain. The frugality of one's life span is grist to the mill of despair and mixed metaphors. Our days are numbered and the sun goeth down faster and faster in spirals of uncertainty. Ask not what your country... After all, there is nothing to fear but fear itself. Come unto me all ye that travail and are heavy laden and I will refresh you. If—when all those about you are losing their cool—you can keep yours and grab an Uzi and mow them all down. And then you will be a man, my son.

If I can be of any assistance to you, please do call upon your friend John.

Also,

I am the whisper in the classroom you do not hear
but seeps into your memory unknown.

I am the rattle of the dry October leaves,
whistling gently while you sleep and dream
in the deep evening.

I am the odor of the carnation you dreamed of once.

I am the silence of the still water
in the deep blue lake.

Carnation, sleep and dream.
The horse won't drink from the stream.
I am the sound of the Besserafian cordophone harp,
while no one plays upon its strings.
Shall we go then, down to the banks of the Styx
and gaze lovingly at the far bank, but not cross?

I am the sound of the dust under your back porch,
where the wind does not blow.

I am the noise the goldfish make
when they think in your golden bowl.

I am the music you make
when you change your mind.

I am the sound of forgotten algebraic formulae.

I am the sound of the hairs on the tail of the Sphinx,
feathers on the wings of the turkey

VULTURE.

Carnation, sleep and dream.
The horse won't drink from the stream.

interview with john fahey

by thomas marney in salem, oregon

T.M.: Mr. Fahey, I was wondering if you could tell us your impressions of Salem, Oregon, and the Williamite Valley in general.

J.F.: Sure thing. You know what Williamite means in Aboriginal?

T.M.: No, I'm afraid I don't.

J.F.: It means Valley of Sickness and Death. Put that in your pipe and smoke it.

T.M.: If that's what this valley means to you, why do you stay here?

J.F.: I'd bet you'd really like to know the answer to that question wouldn't you, you failing old blue Jag?

T.M.: Yes, I certainly would.

J.F.: OK, look. My mother was a piano teacher. She knew lots of piano teachers.

T.M.: Right.

J.F.: One of the piano teachers she knew was Duke Ellington's mother. Most people don't know it, but the Duke was from D.C. I was a precocious kid and didn't want to learn a bunch of schmaltz from my mother, so she fixed me up with Mrs. Ellington.

T.M.: And?

J.F.: Mrs. Ellington made me do Czerny, Bach, and Mikrokosmos. She said she might teach me something about jazz if I studied those other guys hard enough. So that's what I did. I studied those guys till it was coming out of my ears. Mrs. Ellington then conceded to teach me a little about jazz. Actually, she taught me a lot. On two occasions she got her son to give me short lessons. OK. I arrived in Salem in 1981. First I met Harvey Gurletz. Very nice guy. Then I met John Doan. Very nice guy. Plays great classical guitar. These and others invited me to various parties where various miscellaneous would-be musicians congregated. There was this one jazz player—he was really good. All the others I heard around here played the worst, most eclectic, unbearable, mixed-generation kitsch I had every heard anywhere. And none of them knew it. They all thought they were great. It's OK in my book to be stupid, but somebody who is reminded and thinks he or she is brilliant, that's too much. I had to leave these parties early in order to avoid throwing up. And all these wannabes supported each other in their ignorance and pride and propped each other up by telling one another they were great:

THE BANDWAGON EFFECT

Now, don't get me wrong. When I say I don't like this or that person's music, it is not very important, except to the deviant inner circle. Because I do not like very much music. I can't stand the Beatles or Bob Dylan or Madonna or Elvis or Leo K., or any provincial or national popular musicians. Who do I like that's current? Sometimes I like Sonic Youth and some of the individual members' stuff, some of Loren's stuff.

It all sucks.

And the stuff I was hearing at these stupid parties wasn't much worse than the Beatles. The music department at Williamite U. was turning out mediocrity and disasters. Why was all this the case? Was there something in the water?

T.M.: Are you saying that the people around here don't have any talent?

J.F.: No. I am not saying that. I don't believe there is such a thing as talent. There are three things, however, which are necessary and sufficient conditioning for even playing a tuning fork well.

T.M.: Would you tell us what they are?

J.F.: Sure. First of all, you have to have fairly close communication with your feelings—with your unconscious. If you cannot—or cannot learn—to access your underground, no matter what you write or play, you will sound shallow and inane. That is because you are a shallow and inane person.

T.M.: Oh, come on, Fahey, you don't really believe...

J.F.: The hell I don't! As a composer for guitar, as a performer and recording artist, and as an arranger, I don't care if you like my stuff or not, but you gotta admit the productivity of my creativity. Maybe my stuff is all junk. OK. But nobody is more prolific than I am. I am unable to not create new stuff all the time. It all just keeps coming. Most people half my age quit eons ago because they couldn't produce. And not only can I not stop producing, I can't stop changing what I write. I don't even like the bucolic-sentimental-cosmic junk I wrote 20 years ago! In fact, I hate it. The early junk keeps getting reissued because so many people get stuck in a rut in their twenties and want to listen to music for nostalgic purposes. Fuck 'em. I am into the present. I hate nostalgia. But what I am really into is the unconscious. I am always *feeling* the background.

T.M.: I know you were in psychoanalysis for almost a decade. Are you saying you have to get psychoanalyzed in order to access your feelings in order to write good music and be prolific?

J.F.: No, I'm not. It's helped me a lot because I had to remember the horrible things my parents did to me and the feelings I had when I was a kid. I was really blocked and analysis saved my life. But I met a chick the other day who—well, lemme come back to her later. There are lots of people around who can access their emotions. But nobody teaches them to do that in connection with music and this leads us to my second point.

T.M.: Which is?

J.F.: By way of example, I was at a buyers' convention three years ago. There was a panel discussion. I was asked to lead it off, so I said, "Nobody can make any good music unless they first learn to play for themselves." Everybody looked at me like I was nuts. Of course, none of the others on that panel are still working, but OK. So here I am sitting over here with this one simple idea, which nobody wants to learn and which really is radical. Nobody can make any good music unless they first learn to play for themselves—the way they feel. And take a great interest in the way they feel, and forget about the exterior stuff, like their image, like whether the stuff they play is any good or not, whether the audience is pleased or not, and all that superficial stuff. But nobody could make out what I was talking about. So they talked and talked and talked and it was all outer-directed behavior and referenced to appearances: "Does the audience like what I write, what I play?" These jerks didn't know they had insides. So I told them an anecdote. It has nothing to do with music. And it's true.

When I was 19, 20, 21, I worked in a matin pool hall owned by Nick Rinaldi, of the Rinaldi Coal and Oil Comapany. I suppose Mr. Rinaldi perpetrated some crime now and then. He never said anything about that in that way or what have you. On the contrary, Nick had this glowing charisma about him. He was always polite, dressed well, and treated everyone with respect. He was never distant. You could always get access to him. A couple of times I almost got in trouble, but I went to see Nick and he got me out of it. And he never asked me to promise him to do him a favor one day or any of that movie crap. Anyway, he loaned me the money to start Takoma Records. It took a while to get Takoma off the ground, but eventually it started making money. I paid Nick back. He wouldn't even take interest. He just thanked me and wished me luck and told me to keep in touch. When I moved from Berkeley to L.A., I had to find some employees to run the company. I can't stay in an office very long without going bonkers. I gotta be outside doing the job. So I put an ad in the paper.

First day, this big fat chick shows up. She's Jewish and very sharp. Call her C. She wants to be my secretary. I said, OK, you're secretary. I gave her a desk and typewriter and showed her the ropes. And I told her, I don't have time to hang around here, so you advertise and find me a president to run the show and a box-boy.

"You know anybody who fits these categories?" I asked.

"No," she said, "I don't."

"Well, look, baby," I said, writing a number on a piece of paper, "I'm gonna start you off at an immoderate salary. You may have to work some overtime for a while."

"At that price, I don't really mind," she said.

"OK, call me if ya need me, but try real hard not to. I got to take care of other things. Call me when you've got some candidates for father figure and kid."

"OK," she said. A couple days later, she calls me and wants to come over and talk about a couple possibilities. She claims she didn't know the guys, and they acted as though they didn't know each other. Very clever. I interviewed them, some of their friends, checked with the cops and their former employees. On paper, and orally, based on what their friends said about them, you couldn't find two better guys. And yet I never liked them. I never trusted them. Never felt good about them. And at first they did what I told them to do and we made money. The camp made money. In months to come, however, I began to notice that these three all had known each other a long time. I over-heard too many references to things that had happened years ago.

Then cocaine started showing up every day.

What it was, they were a coke ring using Takoma Records as a cover. I kept trying to get them to change, but no soap. I found myself very nervous, running a company of cokeheads with coke hidden around the place. I warned them and told them I'd fire them. They threatened blackmail. So I asked Mr. Rinaldi what I should do. He said to close down the company, stat. Liquidate it. He would find somebody to buy it and he did. Chrysalis. And with the money paid, I moved up here to Salem.

But here's the point. Nick told me, "Make this a learning

experience, kid. Whenever you got a business or any other kind
of decision to make, go by your feelings. Don't pay any attention to the precise. Go for your feelings, kid. That's how I got
where I am now, kid. And that's how I stay here. You wanna
start another company, watch yr feelings for who you hire.
Good luck, kid, and if you need some dough, call me up."

And that's how I make music. By my feelings. And that's how
I keep ahead. That's why I'm prolific.

T.M.: OK, Fahey, you said there are three things, what's the third?

J.F.: Oh yeah. Hard work. Just hard work. There's no such thing
as talent. Just emotions and paying attention to them and hard
work. That's the formula Mr. Rinaldi taught me. And in the
long run, you can't lose. Anyway, back to Salem. All I find is
musical-emotional morons. But then one day, this kid shows up,
Jeff Almond. He plays pretty well. But communication problems. And keeps showing up wanting guitar lessons. But none
of them have that electricity. And none of them realize that
I can't teach them anything. All I can do is help you to teach
yourself. All I can do is show you some tricks which won't help
you much. Mostly, all I do is stand in your corner and root for
you and fight for you. And if ya got the other stuff and ya trust
me to do what I tell you to do, you gotta know I believe, I'll go
out there and die for you if I have to. You gotta know that in
your bones. *Feel it.* And if ya do feel it, then I can help you, but
also, you'll be teaching me a lot, too. And it won't be a two-fer,
it's a one-fer. And either ya get the idea and ya take it and we
work it, or ya don't. It's a complete reciprocity and extension in
your whole life and vice versa. It's all or nothing and we both
win. Nobody's out in front and nobody loses because it's all
one thing. It's all one life—not two, one. And either you want
to do it or you don't. And there's very little I can do unless you
already understand this without me having to explain it to you.
And it's forever and for all eternity. You got anything better to
do? I don't. Fact is, I don't want to do anything else. I'm tired
of playing solo. And if you want to help put it together, I will
give you everything I have. I did it once before when I was 18,

19, with a girl named Pat Sullivan. And what happened was hard to believe, but she and I wrote more songs then than ever after. In fact, after she broke up with me she never wrote any more. It looked like I was her teacher and lover, but actually she was teaching me more that I was teaching her. She didn't know it, but I did, and the fact is, you're already a much better guitar composer than I'll ever be. Maybe you don't know it, but I do. And don't forget when you go to Denmark or Finmark or anywhere, grab your coat and don't forget your hat. Leave your worries on your doorstep. Life's sweet, just direct your feelings to the sunny, sunny side of the street. Pitter pat, y'know? Life's alright if ya dig that beat on the sunny, sunny side of the street. "Used to walk in the shade with my blues on parade, what a drag, oh man, gettin' on stuck in the shade…"

[*]

you are always with me

Dear Dr. A.,

I hope that you and your family and your practice and whatever else is important to you are all doing very well. I want to apologize for the time I was in L.A. and tried to contact you. All I wanted was for you to say, "Hi, John, I'm too busy to see you now, I hope you are well, try me next time or make an appointment, goodbye." But I couldn't even get that. So I got caught up in a frenzy, lost control of myself, and . . .

I hope you will forgive me for this. I won't do it again. I am still very creative, more so than ever. I got the *Rolling Stone Magazine* figurative plaque for Comeback Artist of 1997. I made three discs, one of which was a genuine breakthrough, *City of Refuge*, a misnomer. I wrote a book, found a publisher, and started painting. I'm a damn good painter. Now I want to tell you, briefly, my psychological history, which I believe has turned out quite well—all because of you. While it is true that you and I did not discover very much in our many sessions, something else was going on, which you are probably aware of. I was watching you, learning your methodology, studying you very carefully, memorizing your procedure. Part of me was becoming you. I don't think this is an overstatement in view of subsequent developments. I had you as an ally no matter what insanity I might run into, external or internal. You are always with me and when I have a dream or a flashback, I try to handle it in the way you would. I don't know if "introjection" is the right word here, but that is the way I think of it. So when I moved up here and began to have dreams and flashbacks about my father's sado-sexual seductions and humiliations of me, I tried to regard these items as you would. And while it was very hard work, full of fear and frustration, it worked.

The matter came to a head when I had this dream: I was trying to get the ocean to go swimming and have fun, but a giant mountain of purple veins stood in my path and "I couldn't get over it." The dream was immediately transparent to me, as I'm sure it is to you.

the crystal cave

AND THEN ONE DAY, after reporting to the sword and sitting in formation around it like we did every day—we rarely spoke to each other now, it was no longer necessary—something new had happened. Georgie said something.

GEORGIE: I had a dream.

And then Jackie Short said that he had too.

ME: Yeah. Me too.

And Jammie said he'd had a dream.

JAMMIE: I dreamed we all went down to that vacant house on Piney Branch Road and that we found a way to get in, and we went down in the basement and something marvelous happened. Only I couldn't remember what.

Jackie and Jammie, it turned out, had exactly the same dream. Jackie, who was smarter than all the rest of us said, "I believe it is incumbent upon us to go down there and find a way into the house and into the basement."

Now, it was nothing unusual for us to go exploring empty houses. Nothing at all. And we never hurt anything. We just liked to explore empty houses. We found a way into the empty house on Piney Branch Road. I think we got in through the window. But I can't remember exactly, because after it was over that didn't seem very important.

We walked all around the house just like we usually did, and then we started looking for the basement. In the kitchen we found a door. We opened it. It was very dark but we could see that there were stairs and that they went downward. We looked for a light switch but there wasn't any. But as we got closer and closer to the bottom we could make out a source of light and as we got lower and lower there was more and more emanating from a door at the bottom of the stairs we were descending. We accumulated right there on the steps in front of the next door and stopped.

We were a little afraid.

JACKIE: I wonder what's in there.
ME: So do I.

But we didn't hesitate. Jackie Short finally gave the door a shove and it opened on to an extremely bright spectacle—so bright, that at first we couldn't make it out. But it was a great Crystal Cavern, with a stream running through it. And on each side of the stream there was a narrow path of sand. Elsewhere, we would discover, the bottom of the cave was filled with gems and diamonds and all kinds of valuable rocks.

Somehow light radiated from the walls and we could see everything fine. I tasted the water in the stream. It had the same taste as the water in the spring in Denny Briss's backyard. That meant we were in some magical, special place that wasn't subject to the laws of nature. Maybe I should have been disturbed, because here was something else, irrational, that indicated that perhaps I might have trouble, or the North Takoma Penis Club might have trouble, learning science and conquering the universe like Doctor Savannah was always trying to do in *Captain Marvel Adventures*.

The stream followed east and disappeared under the far wall into a bunch of tropical-looking plants, most of which were either giant iris plants or fruit plants and dwarf fruit tree plants, like peach trees. Yeah, there were lots of peaches lying around and on the trees themselves. We picked some up and ate them. They didn't taste like any peaches we had ever had. They tasted like cherry sodas with vanilla ice cream in them. Wow! We walked on the left path and headed east, and sitting and standing beside the left wall we found a bunch of ceramic dolls or figures. I don't know exactly what you call them. They were little people. There were twelve of them. They were a king and queen of old, wonderful Aztec Mexico —where they used to practice human sacrifices all the time, like any sane civilization does—and their court. The kids and the advisers and the medicine man and some figures which we couldn't identify as to function. One had a tiered circular series of round plate-like objects with a steel dowel sticking out of the statue's stomach.

Somehow I knew that if I picked this guy up and pushed down on the round plate-like objects, I would hear some beautiful music. So I did. I picked it up and pushed down on it. And what it turned out to be was a little tiny record player. When I pushed, all of a sudden music started coming out from all over the place, and from no place, and it was Javanese gamelan music, which was our club's favorite kind of music. And it was big and massive and subtle and quiet and there were metallophones and idiophones and a chelumpung and lots of singers.

It was the most beautiful gamelan music we ever heard.

So we all sat down and just kept eating those wonderful peaches and listening to the gamelan music emanating from the crystal walls of the cave.

We began to feel like we were with the magic Q sword. We went into a semi-trance for a while, which was nothing unusual, but nothing at all happened so finally Jackie Short spoke:

JACKIE: Maybe we were supposed to come here but nothing's happened, so I guess we might as well go and do something else.
ME: Yeah, I guess so. I mean, we can always come back.

So we started walking single file toward the door to the outside door. But just before we opened it, we heard a voice. A deep, resounding, but not unduly or inappropriately loud, voice. And this is what it said:

VOICE: Hey, come on guys. You're not going to take off already are you, and leave me all alone here?

We turned around and there was a slightly chubby, bald-headed guy in a white soda-fountain suit, sitting in between the flower fronds.

VOICE: Ya know guys, sometimes I get awfully lonely, even though I can leave anytime I want and go anywhere I want.

To which he added:

VOICE: Come on, Eddie, you know me. Introduce me to your friends.

So we all looked at Jackie.

JACKIE: Oh fellows, there he is. I've only seen him once before, but he's a great guy. Allow me to introduce you to
THE GREAT KOONAKLASTER.

For a moment we stood speechless, because this god that we said prayers to and chanted to every day of our lives—he didn't look like much of a god to us. He wasn't big and terrible and ugly like all the other gods. So we each went up to him and shook hands with him and told him our names.

G.K.: Of course, I already know you guys real well because you chant so much and sit around the sword and absorb my vibes. But I thought it was time for us to meet.

JACKIE: Sure is good to see you again, Great Koonaklaster.

G.K.: Good to see you, too, Jackie. Just call me Great K.

JACKIE: OK, Great K. Whatever you say.

JAMMIE: Gosh, Great K., I believe you really are

THE GREAT KOONAKLASTER

but meaning no disrespect, of course, you don't look like a god. You look like an ordinary human being.

G.K.: Oh, you want to see my universal terrible form, dig this.

And suddenly there was a giant monster that reached up out of the cavern and was as tall as the sky.

G.K.: How do ya like this one?

Then he turned into a giant dragon and breathed fire all over the place.

"Hey!" we all yelled, "Come back down here! You're scaring us!"

"Oh, OK," he thundered, and then he was back again as the same short little guy with a soda-jerk suit on.

G.K.: Well, Jammie, you wanted to see what you think gods should look like, so I showed you. Don't blame me. After all, you may not know it, but I'm here to serve you, not the other way around. Just keep chanting and I'll watch out for you all your days, and when you kick the bucket someday, you'll go straight to Valhalla and you'll love it there. Killing and pillaging and raping every day of the week. We all take turns. But every day, even if we've been terribly mutilated or slaughtered, we wake up brand-new and fresh as a daisy or peach.

JAMMIE: Gosh, really?

G.K.: Would I kid somebody who chants my name 16 rounds a day and some days more? Oh, I know you never told anybody, but let me tell all of you, Jackie, Johnny, Jammie chants secretly in the middle of the night and sometimes he chants 40 or 50 ROUNDS. He's the most devout person here.

JACKIE: Gosh, I didn't know that, I'm amazed.

JAMMIE: Oh, Great K.'s just joking. I don't chant that much. If I did, I'd never get any sleep. Come on, Great K.'s just joking.

G.K.: Well maybe so, maybe not, but say, listen kids, how'd you like to have some ice-cream sodas? I make the best ice-cream sodas in the universe. All the other gods are really jealous of me because they can't figure out how I do it.

ALL: We were all thirsty anyway, but we all wanted...

G.K.: What flavor would you like, Johnny?

ME: Mmm. Well, I hear your cherry sodas with vanilla ice cream are awfully good.

G.K.: Those are my best. They're all good, but those are the best. And not only that, but if you have one of my sodas, every soda you have after that will taste just like mine do—and lemme tell ya kid, nobody makes 'em as good as

THE GREAT KOONAKLASTER.

So we all had cherry sodas with vanilla ice cream. Great K. had a soda fountain hidden in the peach fronds. And boy were they good.

There's nothing more I can tell you about how good they were.

Nothing.

There aren't any words.

After we were through eating our sodas, Great K. again spoke:

G.K.: Now let's sit down for just a minute or two fellas. I got a few things to tell ya. Nothing very important for right now, but I gotta tell ya anyway.

ALL: OK.

G.K.: First of all, I want ya to know that I really love you and will always watch out for ya as long as you keep chanting. Please don't ever stop chanting, kids. It's the most important thing to do in this life. Will ya promise me, without your fingers crossed, that you'll all keep chanting as long as you're alive? Even if you forget once in a while, don't let that get you down. Please just start again. Don't worry.

So we all promised Great K. we would always chant.
Then he said:

G.K.: Now you may wonder why I keep bugging you about the chanting. Let me tell you. There's two reasons. First of all, when you chant, we are all together. And not just together. We actually are all identical. I am, you are, we all are. And that way we can all be together and all help each other more. But there's another reason, and I can't tell ya about it yet, but it's for your own good and for the good of the whole world in fact. Because kids, someday, not too soon, but not too far away, some terrible green monsters are going to invade planet earth. And we've got to kill every one of them and eat them, or they'll kill every one of us and eat us. And see kids, you're going to need all your strength and all your wits about you to even fight in this war, much less win it. And chanting will make you stronger and wiser more than everything else in the world. Oh, I know about the Q sword. I sent that to you many years ago when I was Quiet. [*] I planted it out there for you. It is a magic sword and it does have powers. All kinds of powers. And it has changed you a lot. Made you stronger, healthier, and wiser. But it's done about all it can do. Because you see, all it really is, is a chant accelerator. What it's done for ya is chant you several billion rounds of vibrations of my mantra. And don't get rid of it. But you don't need to sit around with it all day long any more.

But I'd go over there and sit with it once a week until you're 21 anyway. After that you won't need it at all. You'll all have to rely on your own chanting. And when you are through with the sword, when you've all reached 21, then I want you to take it across the Sligo River into cat-person land and give it to them and tell them I told you to tell them to give it to Big Cat. Because he'll need it by then. He'll need some rejuvenation.

And don't forget to be kind to a cat. Those cat people are very dear to me and not only that, but they're going to fight in the war I told you about and are going to die fighting for you. I've got a lot more to reveal to you but most of it will

[*]

the final battle: part two

ME: OK, Buddy, if what you're telling me is true, you've got some questions to answer.

HE: I sure do, Chonney. I understand that. Shoot.

ME: OK, so tell me what your real name is, Booby, and no more dead-dog stuff.

HE: Steve Wexler, Johnny, Steve Wexler. And it's a real pleasure to meet you in the flesh, so to speak—I mean, without pulling a bunch of tricks on you. But you've gotta admit, Chonney, they were pretty funny tricks. I didn't invent them, you know, *he* did.

ME: You mean Great K. made up those tricks?

WEXLER: Sure, Chonney, I should probably start calling you Johnny. I'm not smart enough to make up tricks like that, Johnny. Think about it, Johnny. From the point of view of a human being—or a dog for that matter—they don't make any sense. No sense at all. There's something superhuman about them. Some kind of divine craziness. No human could make up those tricks.

ME: Well, you've got something there. I never could figure it out. And they were pretty funny.

WEXLER: Yes, Johnny. Remember the time I made you take a can of dog food into the nonexistent dog's backyard and fill up a bowl of water for him, and the lady who lived there came out and asked you what you were doing?

ME: Yeah, and she told me I was crazy as hell, that there wasn't no dead dog that lived there, never had been, no dog house, no shrine of any little fucking holy martyr black dogs and...

WEXLER: ... and then I started intoning the liturgy of the little black dog...

ME: Yeah, you told the lady, "It doesn't matter ma'am, it doesn't matter, he, gulp, my little, gulp, friend, he knew and I knew too that someday they would come along and take him away and that we would never see him again, and it doesn't matter because now the little black dog is with God and Jesus and the Holy Spirit and all the company of hosts in heaven and... and that you knew who really killed the little black dog and then you shouted at her that she killed the little black dog and that God would punish her when she *dieeed* because the little black dog was your, gulp, friend and he knew that someday they would come and take him away and...

WEXLER: ...and we would, nobody would ever see him again and that she had killed the little black dog and...

ME: And you wouldn't stop talking and talking and talking to her just like you did me, and I kept yelling, "Yeah, yeah, yeah, it's true, lady, you killed the little black dog." And finally she called her husband, and she was yelling and she told him there were two nuts out in the backyard driving her crazy and they wouldn't go away and she didn't know what to do and she cried

HELP...

WEXLER: ...yeah, and then he came running out and tried to catch you and I started yelling at him that he was the guy who killed the little black dog and not his old lady, and that you made a mistake and you started crying and shrieking and it was YOU who killed the little black dog and the guy started yelling, "*What little black dog? I ain't got no little black dog, never did! Who the hell are you? I never killed no dog in my life!*" And we kept yelling at him, "Yes you did, yes you did, yes you did, you're a dog-killer, everywhere you go you kill little black dogs, you've been doing it all you life, we know, we know," and then the guy got kinda sad and tried to explain that he liked dogs, especially little black dogs, and that he didn't kill your dog, and that he said it wasn't your dog, and that it was the Holy Spirit's little black dog and that he had chopped his head off and then his toes and then his ears and when he was all through, he cooked the little black dog and *ate him.* "You cannibal!" You kept calling him a cannibal and a dog-killer and an animal-hater and you said "I bet you beat your wife, too, and your kids and..."

ME: ...yeah, and finally the guy blew up and ran out through the gate and tried to catch me and was yelling and screaming that he didn't kill dogs, never, and I slipped out the garden gate and the whole neighborhood was watching and listening and then the cops came by, but by this time, we were both rolling around on my front porch, laughing and laughing and laughing, and we couldn't stop laughing, and then our stomachs started hurting, and come to think about it, that was one of the funniest and greatest experiences in my life...

WEXLER: ...that's because Great K. sent it! And now there's gonna be more, Johnny. More great laughs. More than ever before. That's cause there's gonna be a war. And we're gonna wage war with tricks just like that. Of course, lots of people will have to die. But this is Koonaklaster Armageddon! And Great K. will be there every minute of the battle. Fighting right beside us, whether we fight with laughter or with radioactive AIDS guns. And we'll win, Johnny! We'll win. And when it's all over there won't be any dualism any more! And we'll all go to Valhalla with Great K. and maim and kill and rape and pillage forever and ever and ever, world without end, amen.

[*]

ME: Wow. Just like Eddie told me before he dies in the first chapter. He went to Valhalla!

WEXLER: Yes, he did, Johnny. I knew Eddie very well. He was one of Great K.'s favorites.

ME: ...always faithful, Eddie was.

WEXLER: But so were you, Johnny. So were you. You've never stopped chanting.

ME: Eddie taught me that. I promised Eddie I'd never stop chanting. I promised him that as he lay dying, and I've kept my promise.

WEXLER: Of course you have, Johnny. Great K. knows that. That's why he sent me out here. We need you in the war effort. We can't do without you.

ME: Ah, pardon the question, but, ah, who are we gonna fight, and why, and how many's the enemy, and what are our chances? Could ya gimme a little input?"

WEXLER: Yes, Johnny. It's time for a little Eschatological theology. But why don't we take a break and have some eats, man? I'm hungry and this is going to take a while and a lot of concentration.

So we went inside my beach house and I had one of those Oz-matroids make us some lunch.

• •

WEXLER: Several years ago, an apparently innocuous radio show commenced broadcasting over PBS. Not a TV show, a radio show. Does that tell you anything, Johnny?

ME: You said "apparently innocuous." I assume, therefore, that this show, whatever it is, can hardly be, in fact, innocuous. It, therefore, must be

EVIL.

WEXLER: Right so far. Anything else?

ME: Only what I know about the Krell from our previous fights with them. The Krell can control men's minds so that men cannot see the Krell's true form, which is green, reptilian, scaly, saber-toothed, gigantic, tailed with enormous claws and alligator-shaped heads, etc. Instead, we see ordinary human beings.

WEXLER: Right, and...

ME: .. under certain particle-wave situations, such as X-rays or TV cameras, the obfuscation does not work and we humans see them as they really are. Are the Krell at it again? Is that it? Are they using some radio show to promote their nefarious designs on us poor humans? That seems farfetched.

WEXLER: Maybe it seems farfetched, but it's true. Believe me, it's true.

ME: Hold on. Let's assume you're right. The Krell are running some radio show. How can some stupid radio show help the Krell take over? You know what their ultimate aim is, don't you?

WEXLER: Just as you do, Captain Fahey. Their goal is to pacify every single human being and then in one great feast consume everyone. Every one. Such oddball perversity! It's downright obscene.

ME: You can say that again.

WEXLER: What oddball per–

ME: No, no, I didn't mean that literally.

WEXLER: Metaphorically then?

ME: No, no.

WEXLER: Aphoristically...

ME: No, no, calm down. I was merely confirming what you said. You've been working too hard.

WEXLER: You can say that again.

ME: Uh, right, now let's try and get on with it. I still don't understand how you get from a radio show to a giant banquet. A Krell banquet of humanity.

WEXLER: Oh, well, you see the Krell have discovered some new weapons. Weapons which we humans have invented ourselves.

ME: Yeah, like what?

WEXLER: Oh, just things like mediocrity; boredom; middle-brow, knee-jerk aestheticism; Yuppie conceit; back-to-nature-ism (noble savagism); conformity; upward mobility...

ME: Without the corresponding and necessary virtuous restraints, such as education, toleration, moderation, a good first five years of family life...

WEXLER: Yes, exactly. Let me quote some Clement Greenberg: "The peasants who settled in the cities long ago as bourgeois learned to read and write for the sake of efficiency (in business) did not also inquire into the cities' views regarding the enjoyment of traditional culture. They *also lost their taste for the folk culture and discovered a new capacity* for boredom. They demanded some kind of cultural products for their own tastes. A new commodity was then devised for the new market. Kitsch, destined for those who were insensible to the values of genuine culture. Kitsch uses the debased simulacra of genuine culture. It is a vicarious experience."

[*]

Then we all gave each other Koonaklaster hugs.

WEXLER: Yeah Eddie, you look great.

ED: It's all from the healing power and grace of Great K. and the great restoring powers of his Valhalla where we fight and kill and maim and rape and pillage every day. And the sun always shines and there's no sickness or death and Great K. is with us every minute of every day.

> 'Round his shoulders is a rainbow
> and his feet are like fine brass.
> His eyes are like flames of fire,
>
> His navel is the sun.
> His ears are the horn of a dilemma
> And his nose blows out cool air all the time.
> His penis is always erect.
> And his testicles are as big as asteroids.
> He sits on the 12th horse of the apocalypse,
> taller even than the Empire State Building.

His horse stands on a giant turtle,
as big as the counter-earth,
And the turtle swims in the
SEA OF ETERNITY

Yes, the air always smells of peach blossoms, and a gentle warm breeze blows constantly. It never gets hot and it never gets cold. And every day you're made whole again, even if you got slaughtered or raped in yesterday's hunt or pogrom or whatever. We all take turns.

ME: Gosh, they have real programs up there, just like we used to have down here.

ED: Ah, Berg, there's a few things you've still got to learn. Let's start with the Jews and anti-Semitism and *pogroms*, not *programs*. I know we used to use that word, but the real word is *pogrom*. And this may come as quite a shock to you, Berg, but our anti-Semitism was never anything but a ruse.

ME: A ruse? Whaddaya mean, a ruse?

ED: Berg, from all eternity, the Christians have been Krells. Jesus Christ was a Krell. And the Jews, beginning with St. Moishey the first, have always fought the Krells.

ME: But what you taught me...

ED: I know, I know, I had to. It was part of the ruse. But you've seen what the Krell really are, and you know a little about Great K.

ME: Yeah...

ED: Well, the Jews have always worshipped the Great Koonaklaster, and they voluntarily took all the evil and hatred of the world upon themselves so that we apparent Christians could spy on the Christian church, which until Karrison Geiller and the Lake Hellandgone Show came along, were all under the domination of the Krell and committed all the evil in the world. So whenever you see a Christian, Protestant or Catholic, don't trust them. Not for a minute. They are all under the

KRELL.

Then Jackie Short opened his mouth and said:

JACKIE: When I was living in Valhalla, Great K. was with us almost all the time. All of us all together in the great altogether. Together. And it was wonderful. Simply transcendental. But sometimes he'd take us individually aside and stroll with us into the forests and fields and fjords and tundra and swamps and have talks with us.

One day in Valhalla, he took me aside and walked me out to a field with a lone peach tree right in the middle of it and he was carrying a picnic basket with him and he took a nice big blanket out of it and we spread it on the ground and he said:

"Sit, Jackie, I have some things to tell you, and some good news."

And I told him, "As you wise Koonaklaster know, I am always your servant."

G.K.: Oh, Jackie, you can cut the holy talk for now. Come to think of it, why don't you can the holy talk forever? I know you mean to pay me respect by it. I know that. But what I want to teach you now is the other side of my personality. You got the omnipotence bit. But now you've got to learn the friend thing.

JACKIE: Oh, have I done anything wrong?

G.K.: No, no, Jackie, my dear friend. Not at all. What I want to teach you is that just as you know that I am your friend, just as I can and do help you, and believe me, it is my pleasure and free choice to do so, Jackie, you still remember that first cherry soda with vanilla ice cream I gave you down in the ground, underneath the magic hex signs, in that sad, sad barn, on that hot day?

JACKIE: I certainly do remember it. It was the best cherry soda with vanilla ice cream I ever had.

G.K.: And after that?

JACKIE: Every cherry soda with vanilla ice cream I ever had after that tasted the same as the one you made, O Great K.

G.K.: Yes, Jackie, I thought you'd remember it. And I thought you'd remember to chant, too, most of your life. Hell, that's why I picked you. You've been the best disciple I ever had. You never did stop chanting 16 rounds a day or more. You never stopped.

JACKIE: And I never will, O Great Koonaklaster.

G.K.: Right. But now I gotta teach you the other part.

The part of

THE FRIEND.

Now listen to me Jackie, I know this will sound strange, but just as much as I must be your friend, you gotta be my friend.

JUST AS MUCH AS YOU NEED ME

JUST AS MUCH AS I HELP YOU

I NEED YOU FOR A FRIEND.

You see Jackie, my little peach, we're all equal now. We always were, but you didn't know it. And we're all in each other. In fact we are all each other. The separation is just an illusion.

JACKIE: Gosh, Great K., I don't know if I understand what you're saying.

G.K.: Of course you don't, Jackie. I'm talking about the philosophy of the thing. You need something to do, my little peach blossom.

[*]

JACKIE: Gosh, Great K., I chant and chant and chant, but you just tell me what to do and I'll do it, no matter what it is.

G.K.: I know you will, Jackie. I know it. And the things I'm going to ask you to do are some very little easy things. Very easy.

JACKie: Tell me, O Great K., tell me.

G.K.: OK my little peach fuzz, the first thing I want you to do is to stop calling me "Great K.," at least when you're talking to me.

JACKIE: What? Geee, I don't know what to call you. What do you want me to to call you?

G.K.: Well, you could call me Charley or George or Harry. I don't know. I like Charley the best, but you can call me anything you want, animal, vegetable, or mineral.

JACKIE: Really? You mean I could call you, like, a rock or a house or an automobile part or the Latin word for "so," or even snake?

G.K.: You got it, Jackie, any name at all.

JACKIE: But why, uh, George?

G.K.: Well there are a lot of reasons, Jackie. A lot. And I'll teach them all to you in time. But the most important reason I want you to learn, and this is very, very important, is that I need you as a friend right now. Things are coming to a head now down on Earth, things...

JACKIE: You mean Koonaklaster Armageddon is finally gonna happen??

G.K.: Yes, Jackie, it's already starting in a mild way. Captain Fahey and the dead-dog guy are already collecting materials, and we almost have enough information to wage a good war and win. And the time is not far off when the world will be

KRELL-FREE.

JACKIE: Then all is well.

G.K.: Yes Jackie, my little peach, all is well.

The scene changes back to planet Earth.

JACKIE: And so gang, that was one of the things he told me. And he told me a lot of other things and I'll tell them all to you. But he told me when I got here the first thing we must do is tell the story from the beginning to end. Because you see folks, very soon, and it won't be long, there's gonna be a war, and we're gonna win. And everybody on our side in the great fight's gotta know the history.

ME: You mean, beginning when?

JACKIE: For you it begins the first time the Potoman Electric Power Company spoke to you.

ME: Gosh, I was only 4 or 5.

JACKIE: Yes, but Charley or George or whatever you want to call him wants you to tell it. And I'll have to tell my story about the first time I met Big K. Everybody's gotta know everything. Freedom of Information is gonna be a really big thing. And we gotta publish it in two books. *Spank One* and *Spank Two*.

ME: Gosh, I don't understand.

JACKIE: There's a lot I don't understand, but Georgie will tell us. Don't fret, Berg.

ME: OK, Jackie. But say I have an *idea*. Before we start telling

THE GREAT STORY

why don't we take a break? I just bought some peaches this morning and I've got some cream cheese too. Why don't I go and make us some peaches and cream?

JACKIE: Good idea, Berg.

WEXLER: Great idea, Berg. I could sure use some.

And so I went and got the peaches and cream, the Penis Club's sacred Communion Dish instituted by the Great Koonaklaster for communion with him.

And we did sit and eat.

• •

After we ate the peaches and cream, we told the great and true Saga beginning with our dreams that were sent by Great K., the formation of the North Takoma Park Penis Club, the sword, the magic spring water, our first meeting with Great K., and all the rest.

And it made a beautiful story.

Of course we had not won the Krell war. Hell, we hadn't even started it.

But we would win it. Truth, beauty, justice, and harmony were all on our side.

And so we all went to sleep feeling optimistic and back on the right track and very, very united and peaceful.

I had a dream that night.

I guess it was a dream.

I'm not really sure.

But in any case, the Great Koonaklaster came to me and woke me up so that I was wide awake and could understand our conversation.

G.K.: Now, Johnny, I want you to talk to me just like you would anybody else in the gang. It's very important that you do that.

ME: OK.

G.K.: Promise?

ME: Yes, Charley, I give you my word.

G.K.: Now, I'm gonna ask you some questions, questions, questions, kinda personal questions. That OK, Berg?

ME: Sure, Charley, you know I trust you. Shoot.

G.K.: I gotta look out for ya kiddo, y'know, yr one of my own.

ME: Shoot, K.

G.K.: OK, Johnny, after the war, and I'm sure we're gonna win that war, don't you worry about that, not now anyway. Johnny, what'cha gonna do after that war? You got any plans?

ME: Nothing extremely teleological. I'll just go on playing guitar and making records and doing shows, just like always. I'm still developing and writing better and better songs than ever. I'll keep on writing books, painting same as always, I guess. I don't know. You got any ideas Kelvitron?

G.K.: Not about those things, Johnny. I want you to keep it up. Your greatest compositions and performances are still way in front of you.

ME: I don't know what I'll write about after the war is over.

G.K.: I'll send you lots of good dreams, don't worry.

ME: OK, Kelv.

G.K.: And I want to tell you I like those new things you're doing. The tapes, the scrapbooks, the paintings, and drawings, etc. Yes, when I created you, Johnny, I gave you one of the highest creative scores I ever gave anybody.

ME: I believe you. But I wonder if I'll ever learn to write poetry, too.

G.K.: Oh, I don't think you'll ever have any problem there, Johnny. Of course, I can't tell you the future, that's privileged information.

ME: I know, it's OK.

G.K.: I'm not worried about those things, anyway.

ME: Are you worried about me? What's wrong?

G.K.: Two things, Johnny. Just two. Your health and your, well, Johnny, ah, I don't want to embarrass you, but you need a girl...

ME: Yeah, tell me about it. But what girl would want me? I'm an old man now. I'm tired and sleepy all the time. I've got diabetes and restless leg disorder. I can hardly get it up anymore.

G.K.: Maybe some girl wouldn't care about those things so much if she knew you wanted her around all the time and that you wanted her to help you.

ME: Hell, one girl just virtually forced me to rent a room from her. She came out to the motel one night and started raising hell and making noise. I let her in just to stop the noise and to calm her down. But then she forced me to drive out to this big house in Keizer she was buying and showed me this room and told me I could have it for ninety dollars a week. So I said I'd take it if she'd give me a lot of privacy.

She said she'd give me all the privacy I needed. But after I moved in she kept coming in my room all the time and I couldn't get any work done! Then she started trying to screw me and she was chasing me around all the time and feeling me up and wouldn't keep her goddamn hands off me...

G.K.: Did you ever screw her?

ME: Hell, no. I never liked her in the first place. And even if I hadda liked her, I don't think I can make it anymore. I kept warning her to leave me alone, but she wouldn't. So I moved back to the motel. Now she's behaving real nice of course, helping me get my stuff outta her house and she feeds me breakfast once in a while and doesn't argue with me all the time and always has a smile and all that but she's just doing it so I'll come back. But I'll never go back to that chick. If I ever get poor again, and that's not likely because I'm doing pretty good and I get $275 every week for royalties, if I ever get poor again, I'll go back and live at the Union Gospel Mission even though the food is horrible and you have to get up at 5:30 every morning and attend compulsory fucking Protestant chapel every fucking day. I hate it there but it's not as bad as her...

G.K.: Isn't there some girl you like who might help you?

ME: Oh yeah, there's a girl in NYC. I like her, but she lives with some warlocks and stuff, she doesn't seem to want to leave her crowd or NYC or something. I know she likes me, but I don't know how much. I keep asking her to come out here but she won't. Maybe I'm just an old sugar daddy to her, I don't know. I don't really believe that, but...

G.K.: Well, I'll send her some nice dreams about you and some nice feelings.

ME: Gosh, I wish you would.

G.K.: Never doubt what the Great Koonaklaster can do.

ME: I never do.

[*]

the future will be like the present, only more so…

Dear R.,

Some of the pages may contain conversations with Bob Guililland, a deaf friend who comes here a lot. I have learned the sign alphabet—to show, but not to read. So sometimes we resort to writing things down and he frequently grabs this notebook. I have read a lot from Simone Weill's notebooks and Blaise Pascal. I recently found a Pascal compendium of letters and *pensées*. So why shouldn't I keep one? Sometimes I am too tired to even write in this notebook. Despite the diabetic improvement, the medicine for restless leg syndrome gives me hangovers sometimes. The John Fahey Trio played over radio station KBOO Portland two Sundays ago. The station taped it for us on cassette and DAT. This event was an incredible success. We played great. Everybody got very excited. I am offering the tape to various companies. The recording of the show would make a perfect record. One full hour of brilliance. People hearing the show in their cars stopped off to see us at the station. And no…

But why do I feel this terrible strong urge to work, produce, create? Today I don't feel like doing anything. I am just lying here on my bed, giving the wonderful spring foliage a 40-yard stare. The trees across the street. The maid is walking around the compound. I hear her stately tread, tread, tread, tread. The building shakes as she progresses from room to room with her incendiary voice: "Good morning, Mr. Fahey, how are you today?" I want to say, "Well enough to bite your bottom and consume yr stupid, phony, condescending friendliness. Why don't you come in and take your clothes off?"—but the super stops me and I say something meaningless and sheepish. Why don't you bring some guns in and have a duel with me? Or stab me? Anything, but stop the goddamn condescension at my age. The age thing is driving me crazy.

OK, so time is passing me by or rushing forward at an incredible rate toward decay and death. Yes. But why do I feel that I must produce and create more and more, faster and faster? And what I'm doing, e.g., with the Trio, which is great, I must do it faster and faster and more and more—when in fact, most of the delay is due to external entropy and friction over which I have no control, but about which I feel guilty. Why can't I relax and vegetate and let the world go by on its merry way toward the (bi-)millennium? At the time of the last millennium, everybody was very excited and it got a lot of press. There was so much talk about it. Why not this time? It's only three years anyway. Shouldn't we all congratulate ourselves that we have lived 2000 years and not blown ourselves up with exhaustion completely? I am making music about it all the time. So is the Trio. Why not stop, relax, and unite in celebratory anthems and fanfares? There has come a change in the dominant paradigm. People now fear the future. Why? Because everyone is afraid that the future will be like the present—only more so. Nobody wants to be reminded of the passage of time. This is because life presently has become intolerable. It is too expansive and there just isn't enough money. Everybody knows and fears this. Nobody talks about it. We all pretend it's not even real. Even when we can see, e.g., the new houses they build are smaller and smaller but cost more money every year. You pay more for less all the time.

Why? Where does the lost money go?

To crooks. Public and private. At some point in the past, the white race decided it was OK to screw your neighbor, your friend, your ally, and not just the Negroes and Indians, and so the birth rate of the white monsters is going down, down, down.

Good. They deserve it. Precisely because they made this decision.

the factory

EVER SINCE I CAN REMEMBER, from my earliest years and indeed now, I have had the vision before me of
THE GREAT FACTORY.
Burning and smoking away. Black bilious smoke covering our city, suburbs, and countryside. Conveyor belts; external coal elevators; high-voltage power lines; immense black metal transformers beside the Pensy Railroad tracks with their unit trains of black-gold, led by the fabulous "G-1's," designed by the father of streamlining, Raymond Loewy; giant catenary on top, sucking the electricity out of the thick black looping power wires, supported by the endless cross-shaped steel support towers which lined "the corridor" from Washington, D.C. to NYC.

As a babe,
THE GREAT FACTORY
sent me factory lullabies of noise. "Toot, toot, crunch, crunch, blast, blast, burn, burn, smash, crash, bash, bite, whrrrr, whimmm, buzzz, boom, boom." How those noises deepened my sleep and made me strong with muscles of iron and nerves of steel. And always with a loving, reassuring smile on its face.

PEPCO (Potomac Electric Power Company) did not speak

to me until I was 2 or 3 years old. In a quiet, deep, and rumbled voice:

"Do not fear, my son. I am your real father and your mother is the Potomac River. You are fully human, however. You are our love child. We placed you with the beings who call themselves your parents, Mom & Dad. But they are not your true parents, my son. They are not even human beings."

"They're not human beings?" I asked.

"No, my son, they are Krell, from the planet Arcturus. You see them as human beings, but that is because they can disguise themselves by confusing the minds of men so that you cannot see their true form."

"What do they really look like, great father?"

"They are all in excess of 12 feet tall, they have green reptilian skin, sharp teeth, claws, and they have tails."

"Even my parents look like that?" I asked.

"Indeed, my son, if you could see them as they really are, you would receive quite a shock. They have neon-red eyes, too, and they can see in the dark, and someday they plan to eat you, just as they plan to eat the entire human race."

"What?"

"Yes, my son. Their goal is too eat you. But do not fear. I will protect you from their perverse appetites and later in life, I will ... I'll come back to that later. But you have a great mission to perform. Your destiny is glorious. You will be a great hero, my son, because you will destroy

THE KRELL.

"Me?"

"Yes, my son. It is written that you are the chosen one, the anointed one, you, with the help of

THE GREAT KOONAKLASTER

bless his great name, will save the human race and defeat the Krell. But do not let these matters concern you, my son—your mother and I placed you with very hungry Krell, Krell who will raise you healthy and happy so that when the time comes to consume you, you will taste better than all the other human beings. You see, the

Krell regard you as the chosen one also."

"But that sounds like Persian dualism, great father. Man-ichæism."

"Yes, my son, it was the Krell who started dualism among the Parsees of India. Absolute good and absolute evil, no shades of gray, when in fact all things are a mixture of light and dark-ness, fire and water, earth and air, truth and falsehood—except of course, the disciplines of math and logic. Yes, all things are shades of gray. Only the Great Koonaklaster is all good. But of course Great K. created the land between the Potomac and the Suspoenanna Rivers. Koonaklaster land. Great K. created your mother. Great K. created your father. And it was Great K. who made it possible for your mother and I to create you. And it was *he* who created your destiny to conquer the Krell. Great K. is sick to death of the gastronomic machinations of the Krell. But fear not, for it is written that you shall destroy the Krell and make the world safe for monism."

"Gosh," I said.

"Do not fear, my son. Now I sing you a song of the great Kantaliver. Sleep peacefully, my son. The Great Koonaklaster and I, PEPCO, are with you, always."

twilight time radio hour

BACKROUND MUSIC: "Please play 'Twilight Time' quietly in the backround. Play the 19? recording by the Harmonicats. That's the one we had around the house. And then at the end, play about a minute of Duke Ellington's Victor recording of 'Blue Indigo' and slowly fade out while gently hitting some chime stops on the electronic Kelvinator studio organ. Thank you so much. I am Ernest Chappel, the announcer. Good night, all."

In the fall, when the sun is going down, you can sight it many days by looking straight down west on University Boulevard. Around four corners. You can smell pork and firewood drifting through the twilight air and the church bells are ringing. A beautiful time of day. This is the hour when men come home from work. And they come home and make love to their wives—and to each other's wives sometimes. Everybody knows about that. It's no secret. But there's more. For this is the incest hour. Fathers come home to daughters and sons—and do things to them. And what is the secret? The secret? The secret?

The secret is that everybody—really everybody, yes, everybody—really knows all about it, or something about it, but nobody tries to stop it. Nobody fights or talks about it. And the reason why is because the church, the school, the supermarket—all institutions—teach that it is a far greater sin to talk about incest than to commit it. Or condone it. "Remember the Fourth Commandment."

Yes, this is the incest hour, as the sun sinks lower and lower and the lights go off before dinner—that's when they get you—and nobody can see what's going on in there and he comes in the room and up to your crib, you hear the sound of a zipper, smell the strong, alien odor, and that's when, "Chonney…"

—THEN—

PICTURE: Munch's "The Scream"
CAPTION: Pedestrian crossing the third and brand-new Carroll Avenue Bridge.

Well, here it is. It's time.
The primordial turtle is going to speak
and reveal his true identity.
This is the really bad part of the book.
I'm OK now.

But these things really happened
and you have to know them too.
I'll make it as short as possible.

the brain of the purple mountain

I HAD A DREAM SEVERAL YEARS AGO. There was a giant mountain sticking straight up into the sky to the east of the New Hampshire Avenue Valley. A giant red mountain. Full of lattice-like work of gigantic bulging purple blood veins. I wanted to go east of it and travel to the ocean and go for a swim and sun myself but

I COULDN'T GET OVER IT.

The name I gave the dream was "The Brain of the Purple Mountain"—a song by Leo Kottke. During the dream, as I walked along the avenue, I could hear Leo's song everywhere I went as I looked for a way through. But there wasn't one, and I couldn't get over it. I was about 40 when I had this dream. I began thinking about it and trying to interpret it. Not a very tough job since the meaning is so utterly unambiguous. And the latent content is so similar, at least visually, to the manifest content.

ANONYMOUS VOICE: Chonney, I have a request from my boss to bring back a memory you've forgotten.

CHONNEY: Yeah, OK. But who the hell are you?

?: You know, Chonney, I've wondered about that myself. Really, I have. I've never been able to figure it out. I only appear on this show twice, here and on page _____. But I've got work to do, Chonney. Now listen carefully, very carefully.

CHONNEY: Do I have to?

?: Oh, yes, Chonney. You certainly have to. If you don't listen, I'll lose my job.

CHONNEY: What job? Who do you work for?

?: Well, I work for the United States Public Health Service, of course. But who I am, I don't know. But let's get on with it. It's time for you to have a wonderful, thrilling memory. Now think back, Chonney. You are a baby in your crib. And one night, you wake up, Chonney, because you hear someone coming, Chonney.

CHONNEY: Yeah? So what?

?: Well, this is what, Chonney. You can see someone coming toward you in your crib. Somebody very, very big coming slowly closer and closer and closer. And now can you remember, Chonney? Can you remember what it was?

CHONNEY: *No, no.*

?: A penis, Chonney, a gigantic penis, Chonney, closer and closer toward your mouth, and that's when, Chonney, that's when, then, Chonney...

CHONNEY: *No, no, no,* aaaaagghh.

more fun with daddy

I WAS 3 OR 4 YEARS OLD. Many times he did some very strange things to me. After a while, it began to disgust me and I told him to stop.

"Oh, come on. Let's have some fun while Mom's out."

"No, I don't like it, and I don't like you. Leave me alone."

"But I'm the one who loves you. Your mother doesn't care about you. She doesn't really love you. If she did, why isn't she here right now?"

Unfortunately, I believed him. It was a big lie he told. He continued to tell me this for years. This was the origin of The Great Sadness.

"I don't know and I don't care, but cut it out! I don't wanna do those things anymore! Leave me alone!"

And you know what? He did stop it, believe it or not. But he thought up new tricks to play on me in the years to come, never laying off, trying to convince me he was God, that my mother hated me, threatening to castrate me, and on and on.

One time when I was about 10, I went to him for advice because Donald Cadilac had been teasing me and saying mean things to me—I can't remember what—and I asked Daddy for some verbal ammo to throw back at Cadilac.

"Well," Father began quietly, his voice rapidly escalating upward into a scream, "Why don't *you ask him if he* [but looking at me] *ever sits around thinking about cutting his penis off?*"

This scared me so much I ran out of the dinette and into the backyard, shaken up like a mix-master. I didn't use this angst against Cadilac. Eventually, I thought up some of my own. Another time, he surprised me so much I was sick for months. I was maybe 11 years old, and he was giving me a lecture on the evils and dangers of homosexuality. The way he spoke of it you could catch it like it was a communicable disease—germs or pollinations or something. Fact was, he talked about it constantly and had me terrified of catching it—without any explanation of how one did catch it.

"It's a terrible thing, Chonney. I had this friend named Paul in school, and he was the nicest guy. But he got it, and I felt *soooo* bad, see, because he had been my friend for so long. But there was nothing I could do to help him. Once they get it, it can't be cured."

On the surface, everyone, including myself, thought he knew what he was talking about whenever he said anything about diseases, health, etc., since he was a big wheel in the

UNITED STATES PUBLIC HEALTH SERVICE,

ROCKVILLE, MD

personnel administration. He hired and fired doctors and psychiatrists, he said, and therefore, he knew more than them. A surface reasonableness. Oh yes.

"Yes, poor Paul, a terrible thing to happen to such a nice guy. And all these kids around here—they're all queers. Every one of them. Especially Eddie and Larry. They're sure gonna be sorry someday if they don't wake up and get straight. So, you be careful and watch out, or you'll catch it too."

It was no use telling him again that none of us kids had caught this disease. Father preferred to think this way. "Yes, a terrible thing," he preached on. "Of course, sometimes it can be cured. Some of them do get over it.

TAKE YOURSELF FOR EXAMPLE.
IT'S NOT REALLY SO BAD.
YOU AND I USED TO DO IT.
WHEN YOU WERE YOUNG."

I started to rise involuntarily out of my seat.

"Me? You? What are you talking about? We never..."

"Oh, yes we did. I was there, Charley."

"NO!"

"YES. You probably don't remember..."

But now I was beginning to remember.

"One time you got so sick and had such a high fever...well, I had to do something. You might have died if you didn't stop crying. Some kids die that way, I was only trying to help ya."

"No, no," but I could see it in my head.

"And you liked it so much."

"NO."

"Yes, so for a while we kept on doing it. I didn't mind helping you. It made you feel so good. But I did worry that you would become a queer, and..."

I was remembering more and more. I even remembered remembering before and then forgetting. For weeks, maybe months, I had this picture in my head and I couldn't erase it. I told Eddie and Larry what my father had said but Eddie insisted, "Oh, your father's crazy. Just plain crazy. He's always saying things like that just to freak you out. He likes to scare people."

"But I remember. I can see it in my head."

"That's your imagination, Berg. You've got a tremendous imagination. We all know that. Your father's a sadist. He likes to scare people and hurt people. He's crazy as hell. But if you don't pay any attention to him and don't believe any of these crazy things he makes up, then he can't hurt you. You can forget what he said. It's not real, Berg. It's not real."

But I knew. He had gotten me again. His brain came around the corner from the other side and got me when I wasn't looking. He was good at that. And fast. He made the past come in from the future and the present. He could do anything. And he did things nobody else could do. But within a few months, I had forgotten it all again. I would not recall anything again until I was about 40.

• •

Radio Station WARL, Arlington, VA.

THE LITTLE BOY AND THE DREADFUL CROCODILE

O pedophile rhymes with crocodile
But if you see one, watch out for that terrible smile
Although they are not the same at all.
The pedophile is the bogeyman (2)
The bogeyman and Red Riding Hood's wolf, too.
Catamite rhymes with dynamite
Though they are not the same
And are not equated.

And rapist rhymes with papist
They cannot be compared
Even though the contrary be declared
The bogeyman is a pedophile (2)
And the wolf in Red Riding Hood, too.

Oh, it's so hard
To be the chile
Of a great big reptile
Who cannot smile.

And it's hard for me to smile
'Cause Daddy's a reptile.

Oh, Daddy, why did you love little boys?
Was it because of the sounds they made
When you found them alone at twilight?

After a long hard day at the office?
A long drive home.

Mom's in the kitchen and she doesn't know.
You have all our love and trust.
And now, Daddy, come to me.
I won't cry if it hurts,
I won't say no.

Don't go yet, Daddy, it's alright, not your fault,
Please don't go
I love you so.

Make the great winds blow,
The giant waters flow.

The great tree, before me,
Divine eternity, can't you see?
Don't worry about Mom.
She may suspect,
She won't inspect.
Please get a bomb
And throw it at Mom.

She doesn't love me, you told me.
She never plays with me the way you do.
Stay with me, just me,
'Cause you showed me this new way to play.
You're the only one for me, Dad.
The only one for me.

By the Homophobia Bros. and
the Purple-Veined Mountain Boys,
ASP (American Society of Pedophiles)
Record number 13157

• •

BACKROUND MUSIC—FOREGROUND MUSIC

Stop reading. Please, I beg you.
One moment for a musical elegy!!!
Something important and wonderful
has died. I want to make sure you
notice and understand it.
You may not have noticed, but by reading
only this far—you may have been irrevocably
changed and there is no turning back.

Just like those radio shows I heard.
This is a radio show I told you.
Maybe you didn't believe me.

I hope you do now. You can recover.
You'll never be the same, but you can get OK.
Follow my instructions and finish the book.
Every last word. Every last note.
I promise you, if you do these things
you'll be OK. Different, but OK.

Now play the final movement of the Messiaen piece.
Play it for the Death of our Cell and the death
of your old self.
For your perseverance so far,
I want to thank you both for my self
and the many who couldn't be here tonight.
Something big is coming, and so far, we have been
dealing mostly with screen memories.
For now, just listen to the quartet.
Later, you'll need it.

Thank you,
The announcer

*until i learn
your name again,
i'm calling you zaihro*

Dear Zaihro,

You cashed my checks this morning. I asked you if you wanted me to make a tape for you, and you told me your name. I came home and started making tapes for you. I have a DAT machine here so I make professional recordings right here in my room. Then I master them for CDs in South Salem, I think the place is called Skyline Mastering Lab. The engineer there named Tom understands my stuff better than any other engineer I have ever used anywhere. Anyway, I started recording some new stuff. Very good stuff. One song is about you but I got so carried away I forgot your name and now I can't find the receipt you gave me. So until I learn your name again, I am calling you

ZAIHRO

which is blues dialect for "fair one," from Welsh. I wonder how that happened?

Welsh?

How many black people speak Welsh? Anyway, that's what I was taught at UCLA while I was getting an M.A. My M.A. thesis, "Charley Patton," was published in _____. I seem to be rambling, free-associating.

I am taping you some new music by others and some old music I recorded. Some of these people taught me runs and riffs along the way and/or influenced me a great deal.

APOCALYPTIC INDELICACIES TAPE #4

1) Noise collage and "Chelsey Silver Please Come Home" from *City of Refuge*. She was a band chick that used to hang out with a tentative crowd at Value Village and West Salem Station. She asked me to write a song for her. She disappeared, too.
2) Frank Hutchison–"Cannonball Blues."
3) Humorous Dialogue—can't find reference.
4) F.H.–"Worried Blues" (1927). You can probably see the relationship between this song, which I learned from his record, and #1.
5) John Lee Hooker—very nice and very intelligent.
6) Julius Daniels–"99 Year Blues" (1928). Played at juke joints along Lee Highway (29-211) in Virginia, D.C., and possibly MD.
7) Stan Kenton–"Artistry Jumps." Kenton and Bola Sete de Andrade were jazz and Bossa Nova influences on me. Bola Sete was a good friend and we gave each other lessons.
8) Kenton–"September Song." Hint. (Will you marry me? I am very sad because I have no wife and no heir.) Kenton gave lessons to my friend Terry Robb. (Do you want me to see the government get all my money and royalties? *Help!!* I'd much rather you got them. I'm very easy to get along with.)
9) "Little Hat" Jones, Texas –"Bye Bye Baby Blues."
10) Evans and McLain (Knoxville, TN, very heavyweight secular song about Death)–"6 White Horses" (1935-36).

11) The Stanley Bros.–"The Fields Have Turned Brown."
Early Bluegrass, story of my life.

12) Me–"Faith Slumbers Eternally." I wrote this upon discovering
that Faith Sandoval of Mazzy Star is on heroin. I think she's
the greatest vocalist of the 20th Century. Too bad she won't
live very long.

13) Me again. Collage: "The Dance of the Cat People"—recorded
today.

14) "Zairoh (or whatever your name is)"—Obviously a love song. I
don't know about cat people, though. Do you?

15) 1&12 reprise

16) "Indian Pacific R.R. Blues"

17) "Hawaiian Two-Step"

18 "Candy Man"

19) Medley: "Silver Belle/Cheyenne"

20) "Twilight Time"—2nd guitar—Terry Robb and collage.

21) Charley Patton–"Rattlesnake Blues"

22) Blind Willie Johnson–"Jesus' Blood Will Make You Whole."

severely legal proceedings...

Dear Ms. D.,

If you do not return the (1) illegal recordings you made of our telephone conversations discussing various musicians and artists I have known, notably, Skip James, Bukka White, Al Wilson, Bob Hite, Lanny Taylor, AL WILSON, Lightning Hopkins etc., (2) my two blue notebooks discussing same, which you stole from my room, (3) the approximate sum of $300 which you stole from my wallet while I was napping after your morning seduction of me and our subsequent sexual activity, and (3) your theft of my paperback book by Andrew M. Greeley, in which I had written my most profound discoveries, especially regarding my deceased friend and roommate Al Wilson, all of which you obtained under false pretension, promising to marry me and provide me with love, affection, romance, sex, fidelity, faithfulness—excluding cooking. *I demand* that you return all of the above items which remain my property, copies of all tapes of telephone conversations, *immediately*, or I will instruct one of my attorneys to take severely legal proceedings against you.

II. In the matter of the emotional suffering which you have caused me as a result of your failure to keep your end of the deal which has caused me great traumatic suffering, I shall instruct to recoup (?) for the mental and emotional anguish which I am undergoing which will not go away.

Finally, if you make any attempt to reproduce or plagiarize any of my ideas, theories, suspicions, writings, complete or incomplete, I will take further action.

I am quite certain that by the time you receive this letter, you will have recognized the profundity and superiority of my research in regard to various musicians, especially the deceased Al Wilson, and you will know that my theories and interpretations of Wilson's lyrics and actions can only be explained by reference to the Hindu religion, which Al had been studying for years, and that your own surmises and summaries, whether completely original or in part or in whole culled from informants Dave Evans, Vito, Richard Height, Barnett Hanson, and others, are sophomoric, woefully inadequate, and will not produce even a mildly interesting or informative book. All you've got are statistics.

Furthermore, I feel ethically and morally bound to protect my very close friend and teacher Al Wilson. If Al were here, and I know that in some sense you believe he is present as a "spirit," that you pray to "him," converse "with him" for hours, take instructions and receive gifts from "him," you know by now that Wilson would be enraged that you would even consider ignoring my interruptions to your own and those of others, because it is not AL. Even though you claim to be on intimate terms with his spirit, somehow you are ignorant of Al's kindness and his love of humanity and his desires to be good; to bring things together (as he did in the case of CHBB); to promote and induce love, accord, and almost, apparently separate "items," musical ideas, and people; and to support them to develop and help them and love them. I paid his rent; washed his clothes; encouraged him on his career as a musician; took lessons from him in music, yoga, meditation, Hindu religion, and philosophy; commiserated with him; sympathized;

empathized; spared no expense to support and assist him. *What have you ever done for Al Wilson?* We were the closest of friends, spent innumerable hours, days, months, years exchanging feelings, emotions, memories, loves, hates. We had no secrets from each other. I knew Al intimately. Al was a warm generous, loving, *kind*, nonviolent, faithful person. I learned an incredible...

In summary, you may have the fantasy that you are somehow in touch, inhabited, or possessed by Al, or his "spirit," as in table-turning seances. But you never knew him, and I am on guard to protect my poor deceased friend's reputation from lunatic speculators such as yourself and others. May I remind you once again that you never knew Al, whereas I fed Al (often going without food myself), clothed him, gave him spending money, washed him, was his roommate and student for several months, and I must tell you that you are behaving in a selfish inhumane fashion both to Al and myself and that *you do not know him!* And are thereby ignoring his fondest beliefs. You are using Al, as do most religious fanatics. Al Wilson was in fact my guru. I know his teachings. You believe that Al is alive and well in some spirit realm. I certainly hope you are correct on this score. You believe that Al is now your guru, teaching you from the spirit realm. But I tell you, you deceive yourself in this regard. You do not exhibit in your relationship with other *live* human beings *any* of the teachings, convictions, and beliefs which Al Wilson cherished, lived by, and taught. You are derisive, selfish, cruel, and manipulative. You are Elmer Gantry, a liar, a hypocrite, and a thief. You do not "know" Al. Al would never condone the falsities you perpetrated on my person. Finally, the mere existence of the first section of this letter will prevent anyone from publishing your book. You will be reduced to vanity press. Is that what Al would have wanted? You are Al Wilson's Judas and mine, too.

vampire vultures

NOW THAT IT'S ALL OVER, I often sit and think a great deal about those strange days I spent at my Grandma's house. Or traveling around town on the trolley with her,
DOING THE SHOPPING.

Har. Har. Now I know better. A lot better. At the time, I was too young to understand.

How was I to know what was really going on?

We were different.

Not much different than other folks. And yet, we were different, a lot different, from the others.

But I didn't know that. I simply took everything for granted. Know what I mean?

• •

I shall never know when or why the enormous Vampire Vultures came to live in the attic of my Grannie's house. That dark labyrinth, that closed closet, that dark study, that maze of columns and bones and suitcases and trunks and John Mansfield asbestos insulation. The castle of *National Geographic* magazines by the north gable, going all the way back to issue one. Yes, everything went way, way back. For here was the repository of the past, cast-off garments and books and photographs and just about everything in the world, from transformers, fishing gear, adapters, gargoyles, incubators, circuit breakers, automatic spanking machines, gear boxes, elephant feet, shotguns, casings, dummies...all gone now, all gone. Nobody taught me that the past could come back and haunt you, torture you, maybe even drive you crazy.

THE PAST

Nobody wanted me to know that.

But I learned anyway.

And I still shall never know where the vampire bats came from.

Or why.

Oh, I know what they told me.

Of course I remember the things they told me.

Sure. I remember.

I wish I could forget.

Yes, forget.

That's what I would like to do. I would like to forget.

But I can't.

The things those monsters—my grandparents and my mother, not the Vampire Vultures—did, now seem unbelievable.

But I was there, Charley.

I know. You can't fool me.

• •

Grandpa, after he came home from work at the USDA, parked his car in the "garage" and walked past the long, clutching grass in the backyard. Past the apple tree stump, past the new pear tree, past the animal cages, past the electric fences which held back the larger animals, onto the sidewalk, and up the back stairs into the large kitchen, past the kindercoprophyte and incest garden, past the poisonous waste disposal center where my mother helped cook the food for all the people and animals on the premises, past the poisonous snake hatchery, past the craters left by the bombs in the previous second Civil War, past the irrational animal pen. And as Grandpa walked the long non-path, he went

OOMP PA OOMP PA OOM PA OOM PA.

And he also went

CRUNCH CRUNCH CRUNCH CRUNCH.

Filled with self-importance, filled with self-servingness, self-righteousness, filled with the despair of the family and animal husbandry life and all its responsibilities, Grandpa went

OOMPA OOMPA OOMPA OOMPA

yearning, ingenuously, for the West Virginia hills where he was born and raised, always talking about those goddamn West Virginia hills, again and again and again, all the way home, yearning to get away from US, his family, and go back to the forests of vines and trees and co-mingle himself with

NATURE.

Har. Har. Har.

He probably read too much Emerson as a youth.

That can be dangerous.

What Emerson, Thoreau, Channing, Hitler, Roy Harris, Aaron Copland, Charles Ives, and those goddamn regionalist painters that hung around Stone City, Iowa, and Manning, and all those goddamn Hudson River School painters, we now know, of course, what it was they really wanted to do out there in

NATURE.

And they didn't like people. Don't let anybody fool you. They hated people. They were afraid of people. People, after all, are a lot of trouble. People are messy. They do not think or act symmetrically or reciprocally, nor in a straightforward manner. They are not clean and are always leaving trash all over the place, always shooting at each other, always coming up to you and saying things like "Hello," or "Read any good books lately?" or something unintelligible regarding "last night's football [or soccer or baseball] game," or...

You know what I mean.

People are unpredictable.

And being unpredictable, they are forever ungovernable.

A cow or a lamprey or a porcupine or a badger or even a
WOLVERINE
they, at least, have a limited inventory of activities. And who gives
a fuck what a sturgeon is thinking about way down there at the
bottom of the river, scooping up all those culinary delights? I
mean, who cares? Really.

Now take a rooster. How many things can a rooster do? A
rooster can crow or he can strut around the barnyard or peck at
the feed on the ground or go to sleep or do the hoobala boobala or
watch some hen poop and then he can die.

Right?

What the hell else can a goddamn rooster do? You tell me.

What can an alligator garfish do? Nobody cares what he thinks.
Nobody. But what can he do?

An alligator garfish can swim, breathe, eat, sleep, bite, reproduce, poop, and die.

See what I mean? It's really very simple.

Animals and plants are easy to manage.

And animals don't make waves. Animals don't bring about in-
novations. Animals don't cause any problems.

But people?

Jesus Christ, *people*?

People are unpredictable. You never know what a human being
is going to do.

Nobody gives a fuck what they think, but you never know what
a human being just might do.

People are just plain unmanageable.

And so, of course, the recent restructuring of society on a
global basis was absolutely necessary. So what if a few million
oddballs had to be offed?

Look what we have now.

Peace, security, world government, world currency.

I mean, where would we be without the World Trade Organization?

Where would we be without the International Monetary Fund?

Or the CIA? Or the Council on Foreign Relations? Or the United Nations? Without Richard Gehlen? Without IMF? Without Kennan? Without the Khmer Rouge? Without the Marshall Plan? Hell, Grandpa was very instrumental in implementing the Marshall Plan. He traveled all over Europe and North Africa for years, expanding our area of control.

Where would we be without Manuel Noriega, without the National Security Council, without the World Bank, without all those concentration camps you see all over the place out there everywhere you go? Where would we be without the United Fruit Company?

We'd be surrounded by a bunch of fruits.

You want to be encompassed by a bunch of fruits?

Of course not.

But now everything is under control.

Everything is all right now.

• •

I'm not complaining about Grandpa and Grandma's public life.

Oh no.

I'm talking about what they did on their own time.

What they did to me especially.

Grandpa and all the rest of us, including myself, practically nobody, in fact, knew that Grandma was a member of a coven. Nobody ever saw her ride her broomstick.

How could I believe that my own mother was a member of this same organization?

I did see Mom riding around on various broomsticks quite often.

But you know how it is. You don't want to think those thoughts about your own mother. Or your immediate family. Hell no.

I mean, I didn't really mind all those forced enemas Grannie gave me on the floor of the upstairs bathroom.

I never objected to them. Fact is, I kind of liked them.

At least as a child, and until I was 13 or 14, when I had to...

I'll get around to that later.

Ah, those wonderful early enemas. Anal orgasm.

So wonderful. I'll never forget those wonderful days.

The three women, Grannie, Mom, and Great Grannie, cast lots for the honor of enema-raping me. But Grannie always won. Maybe she rigged the lottery.

Oh, how I loved those enemas.

But it's the Vampire Vultures that stand out in my memory.

This rare species, *Walpurgus Transfusiomous Invitatsiones*, indigenous only to the greater Washington, D.C. experience or holocaust, came back every night, flew in the roost-way, found a dowel built by Grandpa for them to land on, turned upside down, hung by their talons, and folded up like Grandma's pocketbook. The pocketbook of death. The pocketbook that looked like an enema kit. And Grandma was death. The sleep of Death. The sleep of reason.

The sleep of passion.

Aimless oblivion.

Beautiful oblivion.

How beautiful they were in their sleep!

And every morning they resurrected, not merely awoke.

This they had learned to do at the National Cathedral Protestant Episcopal Confession by appointment only, Bishop Agnus Dung, DDS, Presiding Chaplain.

Bishop Dung wore black and white clothes like the Vampire Vultures. My grandmother wore black and white clothes like the Vampire Vultures. So did my great-grandmother. And so did my mother. But only Mother and Grandma carried around the heart-shaped pocket-book of Death. Mom and I had to stay at Grandpa and Grandma's house in order to avoid being brutally beaten, raped, murdered, and eaten by my father, Aloysius John Fahey, who worked for the United States Public Health Service, Personnel Administration.

At least that's what he said he did.

Dad didn't wear black and white clothes like Bishop Dung, my grandmother, my mother, and the Vampire Vultures.

No, Dad had no interest in animals. He didn't even like Vampire Vultures.

No, my father was into little boys.

How horrible.

In retrospect, Mom and Dad's marriage was doomed from the start. Mom should have married into her own caste.

I guess nobody made her read the Bhagavad Gita where it explains all about castes.

Everybody knows animal castes shouldn't mix.

Mom should have married a large bird-man. A man who was into falconry or great horned owls or turkey vultures or at the very least black vultures or crows.

Oh well, the die was cast long before I was born. Yes. And the cat was out of the bag. The fat was in the fire. The writing was on the wall.

Mom and I were quite happy living at my grandparents. We didn't have to sneak around and try to avoid catching my father's attention and getting stuck in the oven. I arose early in the morning and consecrated the booze and then transsubstantiated it and administered it to the Vampire Vultures in the attic. Grandpa bought the communion wine from a Maryland moonshiner who always made his deliveries in a black suit, white shirt, and black tie. I enjoyed this ritual very much, Bishop Dung had taught me the ritual and ordained me to perform it in a short ceremony in one of the pederasty chapels in the great Cathedral of the Protestant Turkey Vulture, confession by appointment only. And so every morning, there was a resurrection for the Vampire Vultures and me, at which time we all drank the blood of the Eucharistic Lord and Savior, Aslan the Cat. Ingesting our Eucharist Lord gives one the ability to maintain one's individual personality including ego, super ego, and id, not to mention

DEATH, TRANSFIGURATION, AND REBIRTH.

Each morning when they awoke at dawn, after our Lord's breakfast, they all gathered about me and celebrated a morning service of praise to our Lord and savior who had died for us so many previous years before without anybody even having asked him to do so, without anybody even having wanting him to do so.

Wow.

And thereby, through the great sacrifice of his testicles, for that is really what happened on Mount Calvary, he had taken our place, each and everyone of us, all species of plants and animals after we "left our bodies" to spend eternity within fellowship and eternal harmony with

OUR LORD AND SAVIOUR OF THE ENEMAS.

All communicants, animal, plant, human, and anything else had

SECURITY OF SALVATION.

During the day my darling pets spent their time in ritual slaughter, draining more blood out of countless unprepared men and women, cats, dogs, and watermelons. And why? Because, you see, Bishop Dung taught us that

SIN IS IN THE BLOOD.

And so to eliminate sin, one must eliminate blood. And of course, to eliminate blood, one must transfigure the host and make him permanently horizontal.

• •

After I saw all the Vampire Vultures off safely in the morning shine, I had enough time to catch a short nap before giblet break-fast around the big round dining room table in the sub-basement, where we kept the poisonous snakes. The table Grandpa had fashioned out of the lovely old oak tree that grew in the front yard, until he cut it down, was always an object of conversation. Grandpa was a great carpenter, just like Jesus was, and everybody knew it. Carpentry was only one of Grandfather's hobbies, of course. He worked for the USDA, Agricultural Economics. He was an ap-pointee. Not a G.S. Grade this or that. In his spare time Grandpa made muzzle-loading rifles. Grandpa assembled everything ex-cept the actual rifle, which he ordered from some other maniac in Indiana. But mostly, Grandpa made scaffolds and great crosses for crucifixions and electric chairs and guillotines—everything ex-

cept the blades that he ordered from some other maniac in Arabia.
Grandpa had a lot of connections with the Orient because he was a
Mason and because he had been a big implementer of the Marshall
Plan, traveling all over Europe and Eurasia and stupid places like
that after the war. (You think I'm kidding. Look up M. R. Cooper
in *Who's Who*.) And he was really very kind to my mother and me.
Not once did he try to put me or my mom in the oven or electro-
cute me or ram a skewer up my rectum when I wasn't looking. Not
once.

It was so wonderful living at Grandma and Grandpa's. I just
loved it and so did my mom. Ah, those wonderful enemas. I'll
never forget Grandma's enemas. She really knew how to give an
enema. You never got enemas like that around my father's home.
Never.

I just loved living at my grandparents. And I loved them very
much. And so I felt very bad when it came time to dispatch them.
Very bad.

One of Grandpa's jobs was to make a yearly trip around the
USA and visit all the USDA experimental stations and survey each
one. And so eventually he made it to the top. Number two man in
the USDA. When he retired he told me that the method he had
used to climb up there was this: "I always did everything I was
told to do."

He told me that. Many times.

What a wonderful, simple way to live.

Of course, everybody in Nazi Germany did everything they
were told to do, too.

Followers of Billy Graham and Dr. Charles Stanley, president
of the Southern Baptist Convention, teach their congregation to
do anything and everything they are told to do.

What a wonderful country the USA is.

Everybody going out simply doing what they have been told
to do.

Just wonderful.

I remember reading a speech by Martin Heidegger from 1937
during the European de-evolution. Heidegger said, "Everyone

will remain in the place where he has been placed for every one of us has a place. You belong to the place where you find yourself when you are thrown into existence, and that place belongs to you, and you belong to it, and this is a sacred relationship. He who leaves his

PLACE

is an *Untermensch*. Therefore, never leave your place." (Heidegger's speech at Heidelberg.)

• •

One day in the sweltering summer N.W. Washington, D.C., Ecozone, har har, while Grandma was sitting beside her pet terrestrial hammerhead shark reading a copy of *Animal Farm*, Grandpa rose his demeanor from the book he was reading, *Black Beauty*, and opened his mouth and spake unto me saying, "John, I think it's about time we loaded up the car with our surf poles and tackle, and yes, yes, yes, let's go out to West Virginia and do some fishing. I hear the stripers are running in the Ohio River. And I have to go to the Moundsville Agricultural Experimental Station and make a survey."

"That's a great idea, Gramps," I offered. "I'm fer it."

"John, Jane, Catherine, Suzie, Rover, George, Al, Jane, what do you think?" He posed there in the midst of time, exposing his *Aufhenen*, and thus opening the matter up for all to peer. Such courage.

Then, John, Jane, Catherine, Suzie, Rover, George, Al, and Jane said in conglomerate mastiglian association,

"AFFIRMATIVE."

"Do I hear any nays?" Grandpa orated in parliamentary manner, as he always did being a big wheel at the top of the

UNITED STATES DEPARTMENT OF AGRICULTURE.

Even though there were only three of us present, apart from the horses and cows and wildebeests and rhinoceri and kleptomaniacs and elk and bison and zebras and llamas, Grandpa had to be fair and ask the animals, too (this was the third floor above ground, where we kept the four-footed convertible mammals of domestication).

"Animals?" he queried.

But not one nay or bray or whine or moo or snap was heard.

And so I seconded the motion and the matter was floored.

"Gene, Jane, John, Al, Catherine, John," he offered, "why don't you ask your old friend Bishop Dung to come along? We haven't taken him fishing in a long time."

"OK, Gramps," I said, "Over."

"And Jane, John, Rover, Al, Reese," if you want to bring along any of your little friends from the other side of the radioactive zone, ask them, too. You know, like Teddy Zoophilia and Joey the Stupid."

"You got it Gramps. I'll call them and make the arrangements."

• •

Saturday morning rolled around. Our fish-stalking companions arrived early, right after I was finished serving Holy Communion to the Vampire Vultures in the attic.

"Ah, Johnny," said Bishop Dung to me as I kneeled to kiss his penis, "so good to see you again my boy. Tell me, friend John, how are my favorite birds coming along, our soaring feathered brethren?" He was referring to the Vampire Vultures.

"All is well," I intoned.

"And how is my favorite catamite in Christ?"

"All is well," I intoned again.

"Oh, wonderful," he espoused, as he gave me the Lord Aslan's blessing. "And for me it is a wonderful blessed occasion of grace to dispense the Eucharist Lord to our fine feathered friends thus enabling the Vampire Vultures to fly about and supply Holy Mother Church with the blood of the blessed, each night before they, like Aslan, through their sacrifice, give up their blood to the Church and then die descending into hell and preaching to the Protestants, thus continuing and repeating for us Aslan's sacrifice for all men, animals, plants, and minerals."

"Hast thou the theology of this continuing sacrifice studied, my kitten?" he queried.

"Oh, yes, Great Condor Prelate, I studied under Archbishop Creighton."

"And what did he teach you regarding the confoundment, that Christ has died once?"

"Indeed, Great Serpent, he hath taught me that in the Epistle of our ancient departed Colossian, 1:24, who liveth and reigneth with Aslan on high, Saint Paul's Collosians, our demi-Lord maketh thith perfectly clear, when he saith and loath be it for any Protestant to ever make this saying public:

> I rejoice in my sufferings, for you, and fill up
> in my flesh what is lacking in the afflictions
> of Christ, for the sake of his body which is the
> Church."

"Yea, verily," said the good bishoprick, "And with sooth, what prithee is the significant implication, the concealed premise, the meaningful purport for you and I and all the Vultures that go about within the Earth and have commerce therewith?"

"The significance, oh holy coprophyte, almighty condor of Kalaramaland, is that Christ has indeed died once and for all in the physical body, i.e., the Church, but the mystical body which you are, I am, and He is, goes on suffering until his final return when the *unheimliche* Protestants who shall be cast asunder into the fiery pit of damnation and be subjected to all those delicious tortures we see in the mystical prints of Brother Dore."

"Smack, smack, I can't wait to see it."

"Caution, my superior in Aslan, your fangs are beginning to protrude."

"Sorry, my son," Bishop Agnus Dung replied. "It is but the promptings of the Holy Spirit, which is, in fact, Lord Aslan Himself, who resides in us for ever and ever and ever, world without end, amen."

"Great," I replied. "Now tell me the latest limerick you have composed."

The great Agnus always visited on us a truly good limerick after fulfilling the obligations of similitude, simply to clear the air of even holy bloviations.

> *There once was a young man from Australia*
> *who went to a wild Bacchanalia*
> *He buggered a frog*
> *Two mice and a hog, and a bishop in full regalia.*

Then at our prompting, he told us another:

> *There once was a sacred baboon*
> *That lived by the river Rangoon*
> *And all of the women*
> *That came to go swimmin'*
> *He'd bang by the light of the moon.*

"Ha, ha, ho, ho, ho, etc."

By this time Teddy Z. and Joey the S. and all their pet turtles and snakes and falcons had arrived and all of those of us who spoke human chanted loudly, "A corollary of the previous, fond Bishop. Tell us a corollary of the previous!"

> *This amalgamation continued decades*
> *But the joy of bestiality fades*
> *'Tis fine to fuck a donkey*
> *But when you bang a monkey*
> *You're bound to come down with AIDS.*

"Ha ha ha."

> *There was a young gaucho named Bruno*
> *Said, "Screwing is one thing I do know*

A woman is fine
A vulture sublime
But a llama is Numero Uno."

Or in the cc areas:

There once was a man from Cape Nod
Who attempted to bugger a cod
When up came some scallops
And nibbled his bollops
And now he's a eunuch, by God.

There once was a clergyman's daughter
Who detested the pony he bought her
Till she found that his dong
Was as hard and as long
As the prayers her old man had taught her.

There was a young girl of Dundee
Who was raped by an ape in a tree
The issue was quite horrid
All ass and no forehead
Three balls and a purple goatee.

One morning Mahatma Mghandi
Awoke with an erection so dandy
So he said to his aide
Bring me a young maide
Or however many is handy.

"There is an alternate ending," said the good Bishop:

Bring me a young maide
Or a pie dog, or whatever is handy.

"Are we all Red Teds?" entombed the great Bishoprick.

"The Lord be with you."

"And with thy spirit."

"Let us pray," we intoned, and out the back door through cages of baboons and carrion crows and elephants and Tasmanian devils and other familiar barnyard animals we went.

Out on the road toward Wheeling, our first stop was, of course, Endless Caverns Agricultural Experiment Station, Luray, Virginia. A billboard at the entrance boldly stated:

> THE END OF ENDLESS CAVERNS HAS, IN TRUTH,
> NEVER BEEN FOUND. NOT ONLY THAT,
> BUT IT NEVER SHOULD BE FOUND.
> THAT'S WHY THEY CALL ENDLESS CAVERNS
> ENDLESS CAVERNS.

The good bishop spoke:

"Other than female sexual organs, these are the only caverns in the Universe which are indeed measureless to man. Did you know that, my dear catamites?"

G.P.A.: Yeah, verily.

ROVER THE DOG: Of course.

TEDDY ZOOPHILIA: Uuuuhhhh.

Joey the Stupid said nothing as usual, maintaining his viscrage, practicing concentration and meditation so that one day he could become the greatest and most wanted, dead or alive, card-shark in the country. Grandma, Mom, and the others in our entourage entered the gilded, synthetic gates to the caves and eventually we found ourselves walking among gigantic multicolored stalagtites and stagmites and catamites along the underground river that had cut its way through the underground limestone over many, many eons. Finally, far beneath the ground, we troglodytes entered the Masonic crypt. It was a beautiful red church made from a Shiva Lingum which had been hollowed out.

"Oh dear," said the Bishop, "somebody's going to incur the

Lord's wrath for cutting up that Shiva Lingum. That is a definite no-no."

"You can say that again," followed Grandpa. "Somebody's gonna get their dick cut off for that."

"Ah, yes," said the good Bishop, "many are the eunuchs in the kingdom of heaven."

"What the hell's that got to do with anything?" ejaculated Teddy Z.

But nobody paid any attention to Teddy Zoophilia's faux pas. Nobody ever paid any attention to anything Teddy Zoophilia said because he was a proto-faggot and a self-righteous little creep who was always secretly going around smelling bicycle seats and cooperating with school officials and tooling with the idea of joining the Air Force one day. And he did. We watched in awe as the head celebrant slaughtered 10 prime R.C. babies, Kosher style, all less than one year of age, and drain the blood into the beautiful red sculptured ceramic baptismal fonts which were held aloft by a large ivory sculptured crusader's experience on a white horse with baby Jewish corpses on the end of their spears.

Bishop Dung and all of us were so elated at the spectacle that we could hardly contain ourselves. Indeed, Teddy Zoophilia had an orgasmic B.M. right there in the masonic temple.

· ·

"In the name of the father and the son and the Holy Ghost, let the pogrom, I mean, puja, begin." As we ate and drank and lacerated consecrated R.C. babies and drank their blood, I could feel my precious inner vampire jump for joy. I had learned about him in a course I saw on TV given by the well-known John Bradshaw. And not only that, I could feel my precious inner Nazi, who had only recently been born, begin the march of the goose steps. Oh, how my little Vampire Vulture jumped and flapped his little wings as each of the little darlings gave up the ghost. Inspired by this great neclatude, the good Bishop composed a most appropriate poem right then and there:

There was a young lady named Alice
Who defiled an Episcopal chalice
She said, "I do this
In mystical bliss
And not from sectarian malice."

There was a young lady named Lou
Who said as the pastor withdrew
The vicar is quicker
And slicker and thicker
And longer and stronger than you.

There was a young man of the cloth
At preaching was surely no sloth
He advised masturbation
To the entire congregation
And was washed down the aisle in froth.

There was a young choirgirl from Devon
Who was raped in the chancery by seven
High Anglican Priests
Lascivious beasts
For such is the kingdom of heaven.

Karl Jung had a continuous thought
Against which he day and night fought
That Karl was God's loo
The receptacle of Yahew's poo
Until help from Siggie he sought.

But we did not stay long at Luray. We had to visit several
agricultural experiment stations, colleges, and cathedrals so that
Grandpa and the good Bishop could make their surveys before we
could get in some fishing. Now it may have escaped your notice,
but there is an intimate connection between experiment stations,

colleges, cathedrals, and concentration camps. All are ruled by the secretive Masonic Brotherhood, Estonian-Latvian Ritual. At the gateway of each Masonic power center was a black tower, always locked, with ancient clinging ivory vines with black turrets on the roof in case of an R.C. invasion, with frosted glass windows reinforced by black steel.

"John, my little cockroach," the good Bishop intoned, "Inside that tower is the true goal of this trip. Your Grandpa and Grandma and all the company and host of heaven and hell and all the animals, plants and minerals, are waiting this very day for you to fulfill your destiny."

"Oh yeah?" I replied, "Groovy. What's the scene, man?"

"If you can enter that black wretched tower, from which there is no self-identical return, and ascend that spiral staircase and look among the many, many black tomes uniformly bound, if you will faithfully pursue this task and search these books, you will find ONE which is, verily, I say, your

BOOK OF DEEDS.

And in that very uniformly bound, black-hide tome you will discover what it is you must do in order to become self-identical. If you fail, this very day, you will forfeit all chances of ever becoming self-identical. For it is written that he who is self-identical is forever self-identical. Thus the

GREAT TAUTOLOGY

and the principle of the Excluded Diddle. Do not forget my little pterodactyl, in the hours to come, the riddle I taught you:

> *There once was a lonely old diddle*
> *Who wanted to be a riddle*
> *But the scholars were loathe*
> *To let it be both*
> *Because of the excluded middle.*

I walked slowly and carefully up the black metal spiral staircase. I did not want to slip or I might have fallen a long way down. I knew this was a dangerous place because the Bishop had instructed me that if I was careful, patient, and worked hard enough, I would find the solution to my destiny.

But I had no idea what it might be.

Somehow the darkness inside the tower and the spiral staircase seemed familiar. It was almost as if I was in a dream. A dream I had had many times but had no recollection of. I held tightly to the circular rail on the right of the stairs as I ascended each step slowly, slowly, very slowly. Then I noticed that the staircase began to move each time I put my foot down or shifted my weight. Was I in some kind of infernal trap? A booby trap set for me by the Bishop and Grandpa and...

There was no way I could know. Yet I had to continue. This was all or nothing.

Finally, I reached the top of the stairs. By the time I reached this height, the circular stairs were revolving and shaking and rattling quite a bit. But they did not fall down, down, down.

But they rattled me.

Who knows? Soon I might be a skeleton myself.

The room at the top was round with circular bookshelves clinging to the walls and along the entire circumference of the tower's inside. Except for where there were three windows. Not much light came through them. Frosted. Here and there were candles burning. Great candles in great golden, iris-shaped candleholders.

I could see quite well.

I could see the embossed red tiles of the ever-black vellum-bound tome quite well.

Circling the room, I found that there were two types of books. One series of books had titles that consisted only of counties and states. Opening several of these, I found that there were incredible pictures, not photographs, but delicately beautiful painted plates, most of which were of other black towers, university gates, and agricultural experiment stations.

And the plates looked very much like the agricultural paintings I had seen which Der Führer had made.

Very similar.

These books turned out to be interesting catalogues of the

contents of the books in the other black towers, colorfully written with all sorts of folk tales and quotes from various sermons given by deceased Episcopalian and Anglican priests. And many bios of these same guys.

Religion, black religion everywhere.

No escape from this hateful institution. Nowhere you could go and be free from it.

It was a sickness that every person in the world was infected with. Along with dualism, Manichæan sentiments, which could not be eradicated. Because dualism was centered inside man, not outside.

The other books were identically bound and embossed. But these books were arranged by surnames. In alphabetical order: Abrams, B, C, D, E, F... My name, if included, would be in the tenth book of Fs.

I opened the book. And as I did so, I was overcome with sensations of fear and disgust and loathing and hate and confusion. And yet something seemed to be crystallizing inside me. Something was getting clearer and clearer.

I found my name in the book of deeds and this is what it said:

GO UP ONE MORE FLIGHT OF STAIRS.
ENTER THE MEN'S ROOM.
GO TO THE MIRROR AND
LOOK AT YOUR IMAGE CAREFULLY.

On the next floor, there were more books and bookshelves and an altar.

I went up to the altar and looked in the mirror. I saw myself there quite plainly despite the fact that ornaments of dark flowers were covering the sides of the mirror. Great swords hung everywhere and there were crosses and symbols in gold and diamonds. Looking in the mirror, I began to see a great black book behind my image. This book was easily 16 inches high and 12 inches long. There was something in blood-red scrawled into it which looked like a title for something. But it was in Latin or Sanskrit or some ancient language that I did not know. And as I peered at it I saw from the mirror that all the other books were alive and shuffling around like rodents. Rodents who were growing wings. They all turned into Grandma's heart-shaped pocketbook of Death. They were gradually and simultaneously turning into Vampire Vultures. The very same Vampire Vultures that lived in my goddamn grandmother's attic. The very same Vampire Vultures I fed holy communion to every day. Their wings started flapping and started flying around and around the inside of the tower and screeching and scrawing for me to feed them blood. And then, as if in a dream, I saw Grandpa and Grandpa coming toward me, each holding a mason jar with some horrible black fluid in it. But I knew what the fluid was. I didn't know what it was made of, but I knew what it was for. If I drank one more jar of it (I had already drank many, at my host's instructions), I would turn into creatures like them, evil, selfish, conniving, strong creatures. But I refused, and when I refused, they disappeared. Or did I refuse?

Maybe I did drink the final Mason jar. Maybe I did. Maybe that's how I got strong and evil.

Certainly I believed I could not be strong without being evil. Isn't that the way it is?

But I had no time to ponder.

I was overcome with nausea. I *lived* in a house full of horrible Vampire Vultures and animals of all types, tigers and lions and poisonous snakes. I began to get mad. Why did I have to live in a house with Vampire Vultures and animals of all sorts? Why me?

What the hell had I done to be brought up and treated this way?

I hated.

Suddenly, I turned, and facing all the flying Vampire Vultures and rats and tigers I yelled:

I HATE YOU. I HATE YOU. I HATE YOU.
GO AWAY AND LEAVE ME ALONE AND
DON'T COME BACK.

Yes, and now I knew I hated. That is what had come into focus. And as I noticed this, all the Vampire Vultures flew out the window and all the animals ran down the stairs and suddenly I was alone. And it was as though the animals had never been there.

Then I turned around and there on the vestibule in front of the mirror was the big black book. And now I could see it clearly. I saw that it was alive, a living book writhing around a bit, quite healthy and strong.

It was the book of my hate. Only I was no longer afraid of it.

I looked inside and it was a kind of biography of all the terrible things that had happened to me, each accompanied by a great anger which I had been taught to hide and pretend didn't exist inside me. But I had it alright.

Now I had my book of life. And the hell with everybody else's book of life.

This was me, this was *my* book. And suddenly I knew the answer to the questions which had been plaguing me for years. The who, what, wheres, how, and whys of the giant Vampire Vulture behind all the others. Yes, now I knew the answer.

I AM THE VAMPIRE VULTURE, THE ONLY ONE.

And then I saw all the enemas anybody ever gave to me, dying and writhing around like snakes do when they die on the highway. And then all of a sudden they all went puff and turned into smoke and disappeared. And I saw my grandmother on her gigantic enema stick fall from the sky like a shooting star and burn up screaming as she went down. And then I felt good.

Very good. I loved my hate. It was me.

Slowly, I descended the spiral steps of the big round tower. I can't remember if the metal stairs rattled as I came down, as they had when I went up. I can't remember if they moved around and scared me or not. Frankly, I didn't care. I had something to do and that was what I was thinking about. On the right side of the door at the bottom of the stairs stood a brand new Uzi. I picked it up and checked to see if it was full of bullets. It was.

I opened the door and walked toward the waiting car where Grandpa and the Bishop and all the others were standing around talking about crops and stuff. There they stood expecting me not to do anything unexpected or violent. I took them all out in a zigzag pattern. They acted very surprised as they screamed and fell. I shot the gas tank of the car and blew the whole scene up. Everything. Car, bodies of animals and humans burned up in a great cloud of smoke. I took my Uzi and headed for the Baltimore and Ohio Train Station.

That was the last time I saw West Virginia.

It was the last I saw the Vampire Vultures, the pocketbooks of Death, and the enemas.

¡good morning!

I AM GOING TO HAVE A GOOD TIME TODAY.
You are going to have a good time today.
This is a book about ZEN GUITAR.

After you spend 21 consecutive days reading my book, you will be a ZEN MASTER.

You will also know all of the essentials of music theory.

Let us call it

BARE BONES MUSIC THEORY

applicable to all instruments. After finishing this course you will know, at least, the absolute minimum of music theory. You will also be a ZEN MASTER. And that's what is really important. If you spend 45 minutes a day for three weeks studying and learning the contents of this book, however boring some of the exercises are, those of you who complete them will be at least three years ahead of your peers who do not take the time to study

THE BARE BONES

system. You will be able to sit in with good musicians who have been playing three to ten years. They may be a small rock, folk, noise, experimental, semi-classical, patriotic or anti-patriotic group. It doesn't matter what kind of music your group plays (or you, if you are a soloist like myself), here is the stuff you need in all the different types of music, using any instrument. And, you do not even need to learn to read music!

Hear that? No notes! Twenty-one easy lessons and you will be ready for any audition to proceed to a performance. You will note that this first edition of BARE BONES is low-priced and guaranteed. If you spend the 21 hours and feel you are not significantly better, I, John "Bare Bones" Fahey, will refund the list price. Furthermore, I will be available at   between the hours of   , five days a week. If something I write is not clear to you, I want to know. So call me.

BARE BONES LESSON #1

Konzept.
You must learn these konzepts before you can go anywhere.

ETERNAL SNAKE. All pieces of music appear to be linear. But no piece of music is linear. All pieces of music are circular and eternal. All pieces of music return to their beginning. There may be sidesteps, stumbles, diversions, excursions, but they all come back to homeostasis. In my beginning is my end. Learn these things. Everything and everybody in the universe has a message for you.

These pieces of paper are black on one side and blue on the other.

In order to overcome your fear of playing, you must learn to concentrate. That is what my book is really about. There are messages everywhere in it, on every page. Therefore, before you begin a lesson, pick up my book, for it is my very self. Hold the book in front of you. Now, *One:* Prepare a comfortable place on the floor with a clean rug on it, preferably made of deerskin. *Two:* Sit cross-legged on the floor. *Three:* Hold my book before you, for it is really me, and say a prayer or chant a mantra to anybody about anything. Or, simply think a pleasant thought until your mind is stilled. *Four:* Do not try to force things and pray that you will learn a lot from my book or that you should become a great musician. These things will happen anyway. *Five:* Open your eyes slowly and look around for a message. You are surrounded by messages. Now open the book to Chapter 1. Remember, theory is only a small part of the true harmony of the universe. This book will teach you to participate in the

HARMONY OF THE UNIVERSE.

Keep your mind as peaceful as you can. Concentrate on the lessons as best you can. When intrusive thoughts enter your mind, do not be disturbed. They are there for a purpose. Simply, rest, breathe deeply, and wait until they are gone, and then continue.

END OF LESSON ONE.

the great fun we had

Dear E.,

I am in the hospital right now with a kidney stone. No big deal. We were sitting around the room in the radio station and the subject of narcissism came up. (Now I am a goner fer sure, facing the great round womb of the cat skan.) This is a nice hospital. I am fortunate. Also the Oregon Health Plan foots the bill. Anyway, somebody said: "A narcissist may act 'big,' like he loves himself, etc." Sorry, the morphine is mixing me up. The narcissist is more concerned with his "space" than with (negative or positive) attitudes of the people around him. He is not concerned with having friends, not concerned with making friends, or whether others like him, love him, hate him, or not. He can hardly recognize the attitudes of his peers. He is only dimly aware that there are emotions "out there."

Oh. Pain's gone. I can go home. Fortunately, I have a great urologist, Dr. Elmgrun. Not simply good at performing operations, but a loving, caring man. I went to see him a few days ago and he showed me my X-ray. We don't know whether to call it one or two stones. They are too large to pass. Next week he will meet me at Emmanuel Hospital in Portland to blow the damn things up with electricity or a laser or something. Meanwhile, I lay here in great pain even with the numerous pain pills. Remembering you and your wonderful friends and the great fun we had. Thank you for your truly *menschlichkeit* brotherly concern over me and your interest. It is a rare commodity. Here are some tapes I prepared for you. Use them if you want. It's Bill Monroe. When Bill Monroe ran out of ideas, and his music began to sound all the same, "everydayness," he returned again and again to Negro music and these raw, primitive, primordial sources brought him back to life. When Monroe is unguarded, he'll start talking about early records of spirituals by the Tuskeegee Choir, Golden Gate 4tet, the Two Poor Boys, and many others. Even the comparatively raunchy-sounding Mississippi Sheiks. Once, in a completely spontaneous excitement, trance or aura, he said with great effect, to a friend while Lightning Hopkins was onstage: "You wanna be a great Bluegrass musician...listen to that man and study everything he does."

I'm sorry, I have to go back to sleep again.

Best,
J.F.

afterword

THE GRIMM QUALITY OF VAMPIRE VULTURES comes out of an oral tradition that John Fahey developed, refined, and lived. One of the true "volklorists" of the folk generation, he would consciously replace the f with a v in an effort to distance himself from "folk-ies." People who had the opportunity to spend time with him will no doubt recognize some of the themes and characters in these stories. Cat people, Kelvinators, and Kantilevers—cargo claimed from his childhood—could spring to life at any moment, traveling through religious regions, mysteriously appearing hunched over thrift-shop crates muttering about a "hospital record," or found in a short lesson about castration.

In the spring and summer of 1999 I worked with John arranging tours on the east and west coasts. When he arrived in New York for a series of gigs, he was using a length of thick twine to keep his pants up and wanted to buy a real belt. He found a cheap braided one that fell apart within three days, and as a substitute, I lent him an extension cord that circled his girth twice. Although this worked, after a day or two, it began to cut into his skin.

One night during his stay, my friend Ser and I listened to Blue-grass and country-blues records with John. He cited the author, title, and year of every groove with a laid-back confidence reserved for seasoned music scholars. Pushed well beyond the point of aggravation by his battle with gravity and the makeshift belt, he was taking the listening test in nothing but a T-shirt. The minor coup of holding a guitar legend in his glory began to fade after a couple hours, and with no one to collect ransom from, we sat around and watched him sip the last of our pot and fall asleep.

On the way to the airport his last day east, John suddenly yelled out, "Box turtle!" I pulled over and John sprinted back a couple-hundred feet, holding his pants up with one hand, to move a turtle away from the edge of the highway. A few minutes go by, he says he wants to stop for hamburgers, casually ignoring the fact that he might miss his flight. By the time we arrived at the gate, his plane had already left. I needed to split but didn't want to leave the man stranded in the airport. He assured me everything would be OK and told me to get lost. I walked away and he continued the quest, asking an airport employee where he could buy a belt.

Fahey's lifelong DIY stance enabled him to cross paths with innumerable people, which is only one reason there seem to be more stories circulating about him than anyone else I can think of from the "volk" generation. I add the myth of the belt to this canon. No belt could fit around such a generous fatso. May the Great Koonaklaster keep philologists at bay, may great pocketbooks of Death be given unto you, and may the nonbelievers keep smelling those bicycle seats.

John Allen, NYC, 2003

DISCOGRAPHY:
selected releases

Various 78 Recordings (Fonotone, 1958-1962)
Volume 1: Blind Joe Death (Takoma, 1959/64/67)
*Volume 2: Death Chants, Breakdowns
    & Military Waltzes* (Takoma, 1963/67)
*Volume 3: The Dance of Death
    & Other Plantation Favorites* (Takoma, 1964/67)
The Transfiguration of Blind Joe Death (Takoma, 1965)
*Volume 4: Guitar / The Great San Bernardino Birthday Party &
    Other Excursions* (Takoma, 1966)
The Early Sessions (Takoma, 1966)
Volume 6: Days Have Gone By (Takoma, 1967)
Requia (Vanguard, 1968)
The Yellow Princess (Vanguard, 1968)
Voice of the Turtle (Takoma, 1968)
The New Possibility (Takoma, 1968)
America (Takoma, 1971/98)
Of Rivers and Religion (Reprise, 1972)
After the Ball (Reprise, 1973)
Fare Forward Voyagers (Soldier's Choice) (Takoma, 1973)
John Fahey / Leo Kottke / Peter Lang (Takoma, 1974)
Old Fashioned Love (Takoma, 1974)
Christmas with John Fahey, Volume 2 (Takoma, 1975)
Visits Washington, D.C. (Takoma, 1979)

Yes! Jesus Loves Me (Takoma, 1980)

Live in Tasmania (Takoma, 1980)

Railroad (Takoma, 1981)

Christmas Guitar, Volume 1 (Varrick, 1982)

Let Go (Varrick, 1983)

Popular Songs of Christmas & New Year's (Varrick, 1983)

Rain Forests, Oceans, and Other Themes (Varrick, 1985)

I Remember Blind Joe Death (Varrick, 1987)

God, Time & Causality (Varrick, 1989)

Old Girlfriends and Other Horrible Memories (Varrick, 1990)

The John Fahey Christmas Album (Burnside, 1991)

Return of the Repressed (Rhino, 1994)

2 x 78 (Double 10",Perfect, 1996)

The Mill Pond (Double 7", Little Brother, 1997)

City of Refuge (Tim/Kerr, 1997)

Womblife (Table of the Elements, 1997)

The Epiphany of Glenn Jones (Thirsty Ear, 1997)

*Georgia Stomps, Atlanta Struts, & Other Contemporary
      Dance Favorites* (Table of the Elements, 1998)

Hitomi (Livhouse, 2000)

John Fahey Trio *KBOO Live Session* (One Hit Records, 2000)

John Fahey Trio *Volume 1* (One Hit Records, 2000)

Red Cross (Revenant, 1993)